Black Magic
for
Dark Times

Spells of Revenge and Protection

Angela Kaelin

2013
Winter Tempest Books

Black Magic for Dark Times: Spells of Revenge and Protection. Copyright © 2011, 2013 by Angela Kaelin. All rights reserved. No part of this book may be used or reproduced in any manner whatsoever without written permission from Winter Tempest Books except in the case of brief quotations embodied in critical articles and reviews.

ISBN: 061588346X
ISBN-13: 978-0615883465
Winter Tempest Books

DEDICATION

A blessing upon this book and whomsoever reads and uses any of its spells. May you soon know harmony and peace in your hearts and your homes. May you prosper and live to fulfill your highest potential with courage and grace. So be it!

Contents

1 About Black Magic for Dark Times   1
2 Magical Training   19
3 Crimes Against Property   41
4 White Collar Theft and Banking Fraud   55
5 Police Brutality, Official Corruption and Theft During Travel   71
6 Protection for Your Home and Business   91
7 Problems Surrounding Your Home   115
8 Problems at Your Workplace or School   139
9 Dealing with Trauma in the Aftermath   163

Appendix: Measurement Conversions and Abbreviations   175

References   177

ABOUT BLACK MAGIC FOR DARK TIMES

This book is for every good, decent person who has been the victim of violence, threats, fraud, official corruption or other crimes and is without a conventional form of redress. It was written to help you deal with situations in which every normal means of justice has been cut off. It is the first book of its kind for crime victims and it is a black magic spell book for the times we live in.

When there is no justice, the conjurer can make it. When there is no way to identify the perpetrator by ordinary means, he can be routed out using the often misunderstood science of magic.

But, if you believe that all of the world is naturally bent toward justice, that karma will get the evil-doers in the end or they will be judged by God and burn in fire and brimstone forever, then this book is not for you. If you can reconcile living in a world with such people and the complete absence of justice by simply saying, "They'll get theirs someday," then put this book down and go back to sleep.

Come back and read it when you can face the truth, when you are filled with self-righteous anger and ready to invoke cosmic justice upon the perpetrators of evil acts with all the forces of Hell!

Why is a book of black magic spells for crime survivors needed now? Because we live in a time of increasing violent crime and rampant government corruption. Every day we see reports in the paper about corrupt police murdering innocent people in cold blood. In our airports, train stations and on our highways, we have uniformed government agents openly molesting and robbing travelers with impunity. Official corruption rears its head on every level of government, all of which is backed by evil politicians and propelled by equally evil corporate interests, who by their very nature embody the word, "greed!"

Meanwhile, if your house is broken into, if your neighbors threaten you every time you step out in your driveway or if you are dealing with a stalker and you are afraid to fall asleep at night for fear of waking up dead, you will likely get no help from local law enforcement. Furthermore, if you take matters into your own hands entirely through conventional means, you run the risk of being arrested for trying to defend yourself and your property.

This is why a book of black magic spells to defend against criminals and restore the balance in our lives has never been more needed than it is right now.

The Recognition of Evil: The Acknowledgment of the Existence of Dark Forces

The idea of the world being an evil place is one from which many people's minds instinctively recoil. It is much nicer to think that people are basically good and the world is bent toward justice. But, once you are faced with the truth, there is no going back. You will never look at the world the same way, again.

The truth is we are not alone on this planet, but we are surrounded by all kinds of intelligences, which exist just outside most people's perception. Many, if not most, of these entities are hostile to mankind – or evil.

Those who practice black magic acknowledge the existence of evil. Black magic is the strongest protection and sometimes it is the only remedy against it.

Some people are born with extra-sensory abilities and are able to see all kinds of spirits, both dark and light and sometimes they are even able to see them in a very physical way. For others, this ability develops later in life. For many people, it develops after some trauma has occurred. Sometimes even the death of a family member can trigger this ability.

While there are spirits of light in the physical density in which we live, there are many dark, unwholesome spirits. Many psychically gifted people report seeing demonic entities mingling among the seemingly normal human population. They see entities around and in people. A gifted psychic can even pick up on their foremost thoughts.

Most astonishingly, they may see people shift from one form to another, from something human to something inhuman and then back again, in a matter of seconds or minutes. People who see these things conclude that evil walks among us, not only in a spiritual sense, but in an actual physical sense, as well.

If you have such experiences, you should share them carefully, although you are probably curious to know if others see what you see.

When asked about seeing demonic entities, people describe what they see in slightly different ways. For example, one person said she saw "snake faces." Others see the person's eyes go black like deep, dark holes. Or, they appear to have a black, shadowy aura. Some of the people who have seen them consider themselves psychics, while others do not.

In one instance, a psychic saw a middle-aged Caucasian man's eyes turn black and grow very large. In the blink of an eye, he had deep lines on his cheeks, a bald head, pointed ears and a wide grin, which displayed sharp, pointed teeth. He kept this form for a minute or so before turning back into a normal-looking person.

The author, David Icke, reports a similar phenomenon in his book, *Children of the Matrix*, wherein he mentions numerous people on a book tour telling him about seeing creatures he describes as lizard-like or reptilian. According to Icke, the reptilian form is the physical shape demonic entities assume on this plane of existence.

The ability to perceive demonic entities seems to be common among people under the influence of LSD and other drugs. Some researchers theorize that they are actually seeing into another dimension while they are under the influence. The following story was told by a former drug user:

One day when he was a teenager he went to a local drug dealer, who was, also, a self-proclaimed Satanist, to obtain some LSD. He had a small bag of marijuana which he planned to trade, which was not worth as much as the LSD. The drug dealer told him that he would, nonetheless, consent to a straight across trade of the marijuana for the LSD on the condition that he did the drug right there in his presence. The young man thought this was a strange request, but it didn't matter to him where he did the drug, so he agreed. Once he ingested the drug he was able the see the drug dealer in another form as a huge horned demon with wings, which seems to be why he insisted the young man do the LSD in his presence. "Those things are real!" he said.

Many people we encounter in day to day situations are obsessed or possessed by evil spirits. Dark spirits attach themselves to weak people, in particular alcoholics and drug users. Sometimes they mingle around the person, obsessing them and driving them mad or inducing them to do things they would not do of their own will, if left alone. At other times, they come into people and take them over from the inside. Such people sometimes report being aware of two or more "souls" sharing their bodies.

Many people who commit particularly inhuman acts are under the influence of or are completely possessed by dark entities. A psychic is often able to see these entities around and inside a person. He or she may perceive a demonic glint in the person's eyes or the eyes may go completely black right before the possessed person commits an act of violence or other crime. Sometimes the perpetrator's face becomes horribly transformed right before he commits a violent act.

It is both a blessing and a curse to be able to see into other dimensions, to recognize evil and to know what is going to happen before it happens. At times, this heightened psychic sensitivity and ability to perceive evil can prove to be very helpful. For example, in one instance, stolen merchandise was returned because the psychic was able to see and hear that the perpetrator was possessed by dark entities and was thus able to identify the person as the thief.

At other times, psychics know something is going to happen, but find it difficult to warn other people. More often that not, no one will listen to them until it's too late. Probably nothing else is so frustrating to psychics!

Dark entities are capable of recognizing forces of goodness and light and those human beings who are in resonance with such forces. This is the answer to the question, "Why do so many bad things happen to good people?" The forces of darkness are locked in battle against the forces of light. This is a part of this planet's history, again and again.

It is beneficial for us to understand we are in such a battle on both the physical and spiritual planes, in which creative forces are besieged by destructive forces. It is their mission to try to destroy all that is beautiful and good, to perpetrate, misery, mayhem and death, and they seem to have a particular grudge against human beings, especially women. Black magicians recognize this fact and only black magic provides any real defense against evil. Christian prayers and white magic spells are weak and ineffectual against it.

Demonic entities do not like to be perceived; they try to remain in the shadows. If they become aware of your ability to perceive them, they can become violently angry. If you are representative of the forces of light, they will try very hard to destroy you.

This subject of demonic entities and especially shape-shifters tends to upset a lot of people for no clear reason. Moreover, because it is a subject that can invite ridicule, if not a mental health analysis, few people dare to talk about it. But, for those who have experienced it, there is no doubt as to the reality of these beings. They are at war with us, whether most of us know it or not. They live conveniently outside the scope of most people's ability to see or sense. They are, also, responsible, directly or indirectly, for the commission of many heinous acts all around this planet.

As human beings and magicians, it is our right to control these creatures and not the other way around. In fact, the highest forms of magical practice involve the control of these dark forces. People who have the ability to see them are at an advantage. Those who practice black magic understand that part of defending ourselves against evil means going on the offensive and not simply remaining passive.

About People Who Tell You Everything is Fine and You Should Just Forgive Evil-doers

Most Christians believe that God will punish evil-doers. They quote the Bible: "Vengeance is mine, saith the Lord." In fact, parts of the biblical Book of Romans appear to be a treatise on the virtues of submission to the state and whatever criminals happen to be running it. Many Christians are fine with the present justice system and sometimes even endorse capital punishment, although at the same time they believe the quest for vengeance on the part of a crime victim is wrong. When these Christians are hurt by someone – even when their children are murdered – they frequently taunt the evil-doers with wishes of burning in hell while they sit idly by trying to convince themselves that the universe is, naturally, bent toward justice and right. "God will make things right," they say, "maybe not in this life, but in the next."

We live in a world dominated by these people. Look what they have created as a result of their weakness and gullibility! Every day women and children are abducted or raped and the predators go unpunished. It is such a norm in the United States that we now have government agents sexually traumatizing and robbing innocent travelers in airports and transportation stations. Police brutality is so common that if you tell others about your experiences of being robbed, raped and stalked by them, almost no one is even mildly surprised.

By contrast, in cultures where the existence of malefic witchcraft is acknowledged and accepted, the people are extremely gracious and polite and the level of crime is very low because the would-be perpetrators are aware that if they commit a grievous offense against someone that the victim has recourse to black magic.

If you are a crime survivor, you may be confronted with very ignorant people who think that only bad people attract bad things and good people attract good things or, in other words, "You reap what you sow." This is an archaic and erroneous Christian belief. It is, also, one that has been popularized on television talk shows because of a book comprised of recycled information from the New Age fringe Christian movement of the 1930s called "New Thought."

This book, *The Secret,* tells people that the Law of Attraction is the reason for either happiness or misery in their lives. It tells them that if they will only focus on the things they want to have happen, they will happen. Never mind the free will of others or the existence of evil forces. Adherents genuinely believe that if they think good thoughts, good things will happen to them and thinking bad thoughts will bring the opposite. They believe "everything happens for a reason" or "to teach you a lesson in life you needed to learn."

Of course, this is wrong. It is completely contrary to all of the ancient, esoteric writings and lore. The universe is comprised of opposites as graphically revealed in Eliphas Levi's depiction of the Baphomet and according to the ancient Hebrew Kabbalah. The law of the universe is "opposites attract." This may be why the worst things often seem to happen to the best people.

Anyone who believes thinking happy thoughts will prevent robbers from robbing them or kidnappers from kidnapping their children is certifiably insane. Furthermore, if bad things happen only so people can learn a life lesson from them, then how do they explain the senseless murder or rape of tiny infants?

What will it take for these Pollyannas to see the truth? One thing is for sure, as long as they can convince themselves that you and your thoughts are the problem, they don't have to deal with reality and the crime rate will continue to soar because they refuse to look at the real reason people are the victims of violent crimes: There are too many criminals and not enough justice in the world.

While the Law of Attraction is not wholly without merit or foundation, the fact is you cannot control every aspect of your own life or anyone else's. If someone is intent on murdering you, you will not be able to simply think or blink them away. People who cling to the Law of Attraction and use it to blame crime victims are narcissistic sociopaths. They have stumbled into the abyss without even knowing it exists!

They can, also, be psychologically harmful to crime survivors. By no means should you allow anyone to convince you that you are at fault by your wrong thoughts, wrong deeds in a past life or some other form of New Age victim-blaming.

Be aware of these tactics put in place by the enemies of mankind to try to strip you of your natural powers of self-defense.

Dealing with Other People and Their Opinions

Do not fall prey to people who tell you that you must forgive your abusers or who talk about revenge as if it is a bad thing. In fact, this is the ideal circumstance for the criminal who easily gets away with his crimes because of those who aide and abet him with these sentiments. On the other hand, a criminal is in very real physical danger, as he should be, if the person he targeted for his crimes is a traditional witch.

Christians are fond of forgiveness and turning the other cheek. Some sadly misguided New Agers will tell you something similar, that the perpetrators will get their comeuppance because there is such a thing as karma or cosmic justice. These are all doctrines that lead to a culture of cruelty and bullying with no recourse for the victim.

If you mention revenge to such people, they may warn you of the dangers of the three-fold law and the certainty of black magic rebounding on you. Or, they may tell you should send kind, loving vibrations to the evil-doers. "Send them light," they say, because it will drown out the darkness and turn rapists and child-murderers into kind, loving, salt of the earth people! This is utter nonsense which can only do more harm than good because you cannot love the evil out of evil or those possessed by it.

Furthermore, it is very psychologically harmful to you, as a crime survivor, to have the people around you not "get it." In instances of rape, this phenomenon is known as "the second rape" because of its devastating and isolating effect on survivors.

This is why a lot of survivors will not talk to people about the crimes committed against them. It is not because they are secretly ashamed, as is often repeated by so-called experts. They are simply frightened by the lack of understanding and frequently hostile responses from people they once believed cared about them. It is one thing to cope with the results of a brutal attack of some kind, but quite another to have to deal with people who believe you must have done something to deserve it or that you should forgive your attackers!

Victim-blamers only further violent crime and enable the criminals because they convince themselves that anything perpetrators do is their victim's fault. Such prigs believe they are superior to everyone else either because they are "favored by God" or because of their ability to have superior thoughts and manifest only goodness in their lives.

With their sense of moral superiority, they look down upon victims of violent crime, convinced that they have brought it all on themselves in some way.

The effects of acts violence against you can run long and deep. This is especially, if you have survived prolonged violence such as domestic violence and stalking or multiple, random violent crimes. A large percentage of crime survivors are targeted multiple times over a lifetime. This is because people who live in high crime areas and people of smaller physical stature are more commonly targets for violent criminals. It is not because they are "sinners" or people with wrong thoughts.

If you are surrounded by people who do not understand this, the best thing you can do is avoid them. Of course, this is how many survivors wind up living in isolation, however, this is better for you than being around people who continually re-victimize you.

The situation of being surrounded by victim-blamers, even more than the original event, is the main cause of severe anxiety for many crime victims. Once you recognize someone in your life is hurting you in this way, get rid of them. Stop talking to them. Stop taking their phone calls. Change your telephone number, if you have to. Do not accept their abuse.

The fact is, if you have been grievously wronged, you have the right to seek and receive redress.

If you are a witch, ask yourself this question: What is the point in being a witch if you cannot use what you know to bring about justice and free yourself from the harm caused by evil-doers? It is your inherent right to do so. Do not let smug halfwits and goody-two-shoes tell you that you shouldn't. You don't have to turn the other cheek, forgive anyone or send out "love vibrations" to tyrants and oppressors.

Nor should you fear retribution in seeking justice or revenge through magic. As long as you are justified in your actions, you are still a good person and a good witch. Anyone who thinks otherwise about you is not your friend and is not worth your time.

Furthermore, no one else has to know. Witchcraft is best performed without anyone else knowing about it, anyway, unless they are very trusted and working the spell with you.

Justice Versus Revenge

There is a bias in modern English-speaking cultures that the person who seeks revenge is always in the wrong. Since justice through the court system is often available only to those with the social position or money to obtain it, this belief only serves to deprive the majority of people of their ability to get justice in any form.

There are those who will tell you that real justice can only be meted out through the legal system, that the punishment for crime is to be entirely left up to the authority of the state. Of course, if you are not socially well-placed and lack sufficient finances, you will probably be waiting for a very long time for this to happen. The fact is justice is almost never meted out by the legal system, in any case, except by accident. Even on the rare chance that the person who committed crimes against you is brought to trial and convicted (at least, in the United States), violent criminals rarely serve their full sentences. They are soon released so they can hunt you down and commit more crimes against you or seek out new victims. This is not justice for anyone – not you, your family or society as a whole.

If you have friends who tell you that you are wrong to seek revenge or that you should somehow just forget about your trauma, ask yourself whose side they are on. People who sit in their ivory towers making judgments against you are certainly not on your side.

It is perfectly just and right to perform a spell that keeps a violent criminal from committing more violent acts. In fact, it is absolutely the right thing to do in every way. Sometimes revenge spells are exactly what is needed to ensure justice. It is what the victim of a crime must do in order to go forward with his or her life in a balanced way. It is necessary to the person's healing and reestablishment of a reasonable sense of security.

This is why black magic, particularly Hoodoo, grew in strength during the years of black enslavement. It was a natural result of the circumstance the people were placed in. They were denied all justice and wronged at every turn by the authorities and those with more money and social standing. Malefic witchcraft was their only recourse to retribution or access to equality under the law.

Many spells in this book dealing with justice and the law come from American Hoodoo. Justice Spells, sometimes called Court Case Spells, are worked in situations where you are involved in a court case or other legal entanglement. It is a way to gain influence over a judge, attorneys or other people whose actions are important to the outcome of the case. By contrast, Revenge Spells involve bringing about personal justice. Revenge is what you must seek to restore harmony and balance when conventional justice has been denied to you.

If you are currently in a situation where you are being grievously wronged or are a crime survivor who has sufficient rage within you, you will easily succeed at casting these spells. By doing so, you will find your own strength and healing and become a catalyst for balance and harmony in the universe.

The Benefits of Conducting Revenge Spells

There are great psychological benefits to conducting revenge spells. It is a way of harnessing and channeling your inner rage, which you are completely and unapologetically entitled to feel, in a healthy and productive way

Revenge spells keep you out of trouble, too. They are undetectable and cannot be prosecuted. It is a way of attacking your enemy that is perfectly legal because the law does not acknowledge the existence of magic. You can do magic spells and think vengeful thoughts all day and all night without running afoul of the law.

There are those who say "living well is the best revenge." There is some truth in this, which is why the last chapter of this book deals with putting your life back together.

But first, you have to get the terrible things happening in your life to stop. You have to feel safe and protected. This is why spells of revenge and protection are both beneficial. You cannot move forward with your life in a healthy and balanced way, if grave injustices still exist and your safety and security is at risk.

Warnings and Disclaimers

As you practice magic, you must not lose your grasp on reality. This is a real danger for occultists. When you practice magic, keep one foot in the mundane world and the other in the magical one. Do not lose your balance or your common sense.

You must remember that while you have free will, so does everyone else. The will of a rapist to rape or a killer to kill is not a matter that can always be overcome by magic or any other means. Sometimes if we are aware, evil can be prevented, but not always. Therefore, always take common sense precautions alongside your magical workings.

There are two main components to any situation: (1) The physical or mundane and (2) the metaphysical or spiritual, which involves the use of magic.

When you find yourself in any of the dangerous situations mentioned in this book, you should weigh the idea of using conventional means to solve the problem first, if it is applicable or even advisable.

Sometimes this means involving law enforcement agencies of one kind or other. For example, if your house is robbed, you may want to call the police and file a report. If you are going to make an insurance claim, you may have no choice but to do so. But, bear in mind that there is a chance that when the police come they will accuse you of robbing your own house. They will certainly scrutinize you and even if you can identify the perpetrators, it is likely nothing will happen to them.

Even in the best situations, the police cannot

protect you because it is not their job. Their job is to file reports and make arrests. Then, too, there is the problem that law enforcement agencies have become increasingly corrupt.

Furthermore, it is a general rule that whenever a certain type of crime is prevalent in a particular area, law enforcement agents are sometimes active participants in its furtherance. For instance, in areas where methamphetamine use is a scourge, local law enforcement officials are found to be involved in the trade and drug families have members in positions of authority. The same applies to other types of crime like robbery, stalking, human trafficking, etc. There is no better place for a criminal to hide and conduct illicit business than within a law enforcement agency.

Keep this in mind whenever you are considering whether or not to report a crime committed against yourself. You must always deal with reality as it is and not as you perceive it or how you would like it to be.

Also, as a magician, a witch or a conjurer, you must never forget that you live in the physical world as well as the spiritual one. When you do a spell for protection, do it behind locked doors. If you have people stalking you and threatening to murder you and your family, keep defense weapons handy and ready to use. Magic spells are not a good substitute for proper self-defense against anyone who wants to do you immediate physical harm.

For this reason, in the chapters of this book that give spells, the subject of taking real world precautions is coupled with the discussion of the spells themselves.

Be open to different beliefs when you use any of the magical procedures in this book. Take what you like and reject what you don't like. But, don't be afraid to use spells or prayers outside your personal beliefs. Magic is universal and not the property of one particular religion, nation or culture. And, there is no telling why certain things will work in a particular situation and certain other things will not.

MAGICAL TRAINING

In the previous chapter we discussed some of the psychic experiences that traumatized people sometimes have and the importance of not allowing ignorant people to deprive you of your natural power. In this chapter, we will see how this power functions and how it can be applied to witchcraft.

Crime survivors and those who have been deeply wronged in some way, very commonly and naturally feel a sense of rage. In the case of any kind of violation, there is usually a series of emotional responses that follows.

Often there is a state of shock. Most people experience moments of denial or disbelief because they have difficulty mentally processing the fact that some thing so unthinkably horrible has happened to them. They may experience intense fear. If they have been brought close enough to death's door, they may feel nothing at all for a very long time; the entire body may seem to go numb as if it is not fully inhabited by the person.

But, eventually there comes the sense of self-righteous indignation. It is the moment that the survivor shifts his or her perspective to that of an outside observer and recognizes how wrong the crimes perpetrated against them are. In this moment the chemicals in the brain that have been released by glands during the course of the original trauma work to create a sense of pure fire running through the body. It begins in the stomach, moves to the chest and surges through the muscles and veins, electrifying the entire body. It is a force of pure, hot rage in the form of etheric energy.

The Powerful Gift Given to Survivors

It is no coincidence that many tribal initiation rites include tests of the initiate's physical endurance, sometimes even requiring nudity, particularly in cultures where nudity has a sexual connotation. Such rites involving nudity, the deprivation of food for days or other psychological or physical torments in American Hoodoo initiations were vividly described by Zora Neale Hurston in her book, *Mules and Men*.

Their purpose is to traumatize the initiate, thus releasing certain chemicals and altering the circuitry of the brain. Even fairly minor trauma, such as the loss of a close friend or relative, the loss of one's home, betrayal by trusted institutions, crimes of property or anything that causes a person to feel a sense of loss or violation, causes a degree of spiritual awakening. This is a natural function, which is stimulated artificially through ceremonial initiation.

Some of these initiation rites are particularly violent and traumatizing, such as the traditional Okipa ceremony of the Mandan Indians of North and South Dakota; the initiation of the Naghol of the South Pacific Islands; and the rites of the Matusa people of Papa New Guinea, all of which involve such things as fasting, pain endurance, cutting the skin and horrifying physical torments often leading to fainting from so much pain and deprivation. These rites are designed to bring the initiate to the threshold of death. In many cases, the ritualistic trauma involves some injury to the sex organs.

This trauma is similar to that experienced by many crime survivors, especially those who have come face to face with death, as well as those who have had actual Near Death Experiences (N.D.E.s). These experiences trigger the release of chemicals in the brain. According to scientific researchers, the brains of violent crime survivors are visibly scarred and this scarring is irreversible.

The aforementioned initiation rites along with such trauma from crimes both represent a kind of death in which the person is transformed and their lives are forever after altered. It is a death and rebirth.

Spiritual initiation is not a one-time occurrence in many old traditions. It is done repeatedly, often before some other important aspect of spiritual development or a test is about to be undertaken. These things are usually only symbolized in some modern Western occult orders where they are referred to as degrees of initiation. Each trauma leads the seeker further down the spiritual path and increases their supply of psychic power. This same thing happens to violent crime survivors with each successive traumatic experience. If they survive the experience, they emerge from each event with even greater psychic powers and a greater storehouse of etheric force than before.

This is why many violent crime survivors often suddenly develop psychic abilities like clairvoyance, clairaudience and claircognizance. They, also, develop a reserve of psychic energy that is naturally energized by their emotions, especially the natural feelings of rage they have, which our culture so widely disapproves of.

Sometimes this rage is frightening to both the survivor and those closest to him or her because it is so very strong and powerful. Therefore, many survivors repress it, try to hide it or in the worst cases resort to alcohol or drugs in an attempt to suppress these natural emotions. It, also, seems to be more often repressed or unrecognized in women than in men because it is far less socially acceptable for women to express anger. But, even if you have repressed it for a very long time, it never goes away. It is always right there because, in reality, it is your defense mechanism. Just like an animal has the gift of teeth and claws, you have the gift of rage.

The charge of energy that makes witchcraft work is a very nearly physical electromagnetic energy that is stored in the body, directed and released at a target. In spell work there is usually some energetically compatible object that represents the target. But, it can, also, be transferred to the target directly as well as mentally through telepathy. This latter method is very effective for survivors, many of whom have vivid, irrepressible memories of those who perpetrated crimes against them.

These are the images they are unable to forget and which become the source of great anxiety, nightmares and sometimes lead to the development of Post-traumatic Stress Disorder (P.T.S.D.). So, it is very easy for the survivor to tap into this mental energy and connect to the perpetrator of the crime. Much like magicians who have trained their minds and creative imaginations, survivors often have a remarkable ability to recall in vivid and perfect detail the image, movements, gestures, voice, smell and, in short, the exact energetic signature of the one who injured them.

This energy stored in the body of survivors is the spiritual component to the adrenaline that is released by the body's glands when there is a dire emergency. An example of this release of energy occurs in a situation where you must defend yourself against an enemy who is twice your size and four times your strength. Yet, you are inexplicably able to knock him out cold. Such things are not possible by ordinary physical means, nor can they entirely be explained merely by the release of adrenaline in the body. They are only possible through the storage and release of etheric energy, similar to that stored and released by martial artists from the East.

Around the world, it is a traditional belief that directed rage in a person who has been grievously wronged can kill, especially when it is applied to witchcraft.

This fact is discussed by Charles Godfrey Leland with regard to the "strege" who are Italian witches of Tuscany: "The strege believe, however, as do all among whom they live, that concentrated, intense venomous hatred, or will, allied to spells can kill."[1]

Furthermore, "... when the hate has really been awakened by a deep wrong, be it from conscience or the mysterious working of destiny, and causes beyond our ken [understanding], it is wonderful to see how often the arrow strikes – sooner or later! Believe in nothing if thou wilt, neither in the heaven above or in the earth below, but 'cast up the account of Orcus [Roman god of the underworld] – the account thereof cast up,' and if there is one on earth whom thou hast deeply, deliberately wronged, thou shalt find thy Nemesis.' Dread him whom thou hast struck."[2]

Among people to whom witchcraft is a normal part of life, it is naturally presumed to be the cause of many deaths. Such was the case among the Azande of Sudan in Africa as documented by E. E. Evans-Pritchard in 1937. When the researcher asked how the death of an enemy was accomplished by means of witchcraft, the Azande responded, "...people say that the witch sends the soul of his witchcraft to eat the soul and the flesh of a man" and "the soul of the medicine tracks down the man and slays him."[3]

Survivors naturally have the ability to psychically connect with the perpetrator and a large store of energy with which to strike him down as part of their natural self-defense. While magical training is important, crime survivors can skip over a large part of it because they have already have the requisite powers of concentration and force, which is beneficial in all magical workings, but especially when applied to taking revenge and defending themselves from future enemies.

When a survivor takes up the study of magical training, they will find that the exercises used to create and store akashic energy and elemental forces cause very similar sensations to the ones they experience when their rage is aroused. The entire body tingles with an electrical fire that might be described as a diffusion of black lightning. It is vibrant, dense and electrifying.

Whereas a student magician who has never stared in the face of death must try to create in his mind and body a circumstance he has never experienced before, the survivor only has to try to re-create in a controlled way the circumstances which are created naturally by means of this gift of rage.

Training Exercises

As previously mentioned, this is largely an unnecessary undertaking for those who have survived especially heinous crimes. Although, they can benefit from conducting these exercises, so that they begin to understand the real nature of the force that arises within them. But, there are surely many people who will run across this book who are either not crime survivors or who have not been so deeply wronged that they very naturally find sufficient force within themselves to effect the desired outcome.

Whether you are a crime survivor or not, you should find the information and exercises below beneficial to the practice of witchcraft.

There are many different terms used to describe the various aspects of subtle energy, but for the purpose of our discussion here, we will characterize six aspects of it as follows:

Akashic: It is often simply called the "fifth element." This is the foundational principle of the following four elements and a catalyst for their manifestation. The seed of the following four elements is in the akashic force.

Fire: This is the forward propelling energetic component of the electrical force in the body. Its energy pushes outward from itself like the positive end of a magnet or battery. Its effect is heat and inflammation, similar to fire or lightning.

Water: This is the drawing, attracting energetic component of the electrical force in the body. Its energy pulls inward toward itself like the negative end of a magnet or battery.

Air: This element occurs naturally between fire and water. It creates an equilibrium and a bond between them.

Earth: This is a heavy, dense element, which is a combination of the previous three, but nearer to our physical existence.

Etheric: This energy is a combination of the previous five elements and is very nearly physical in its density. In another manner of speaking, the term etheric could be used to describe all of the previous elements, however, this is not the definition we are using here. In this instance, etheric is being used to describe the nearly physical aspect of ourselves and of ghosts and spirits that are very nearly physical manifestations.

It is important not to confuse the symbolic representations of the four elements, fire, water, air and earth, with these physical things by the same name in nature. These elements are frequently symbolized in ceremonial magic as a reminder to the magician or as an anchoring mechanism in the practice of witchcraft. But, many modern witches, lacking true initiation to the mysteries, often confuse them with the actual physical expressions of fire, water, air and earth.

You will personally experience the effects of these spiritual elements, if you conduct the following exercises properly.

Exercise 1

There are two methods described below for creating the energy used in black magic. The first is the most effective in spells of a vengeful or protective nature, especially when that action is warranted. The second can be used by anyone who has well-developed meditation and visualization skills. Crime survivors will be able to compare the effects of the two methods.

Method 1: Conjuring Power through Rage

Rage occurs spontaneously in crime survivors, sometimes when it is not desired. But, it can be summoned very easily by the power of memory.

Before casting a spell for revenge or protection, all that is necessary to formulate a powerful charge is to recall an event that inspires your rage. Consider an injustice of the past or one that is currently at hand and allow yourself to be filled with this force. Allow yourself to remember the crimes and injustices perpetrated against you.

When your rage is aroused, you feel a surge of energy from the region of your abdomen, that moves upward through the solar plexus and runs throughout the body, electrifying and energizing it.

This is not a slow easy movement, like we usually think of in connection to Eastern-style meditation. Instead, it is a ball of electrified rage, like black lightning, that shoots through the body with great speed and force.

It causes the pulse to increase, breathing may be affected and the entire body shakes. It may be accompanied by a desire to do serious harm to the offending party – maybe even to kill – because it was aroused by your memories of a terrifying experience, which has marred your consciousness with a sense of grave injustice that remains unrectified.

This energy is the killing power of witchcraft. When it is concentrated and released by a witch, it finds its target as surely and swiftly as a heat-seeking missile.

If you are a crime survivor who experiences bouts of rage, compare the feeling of energy surging throughout your body in this method to the feeling you get when you use the second method.

Method 2: Conjuring Power through Meditation

With the previous method, the following steps come together very naturally and the magician doesn't really have to think about any procedure or aspect of the elements to produce the etheric force. The power is produced naturally through the gift of rage.

With the following procedure, you will see the breakdown of how the elements come together to create this power within a person. Each time the magician does this meditation, his or her power becomes a little stronger and more concentrated than before.

Take up your usual meditative posture, which may be sitting, standing or lying down. Visualize a black ball of energy tinged with purple that is popping and crackling like lightning in the pit of your stomach, located right on your spinal column, behind your navel. Try to remain conscious of your breathing. Upon each inhale, draw this energy in and with exhale concentrate it into a little ball in the pit of your stomach.

The ball you are forming is one comprised of pure akashic energy. Keep breathing and drawing the energy in and compressing it into a ball. Remain conscious of maintaining steady, even breathing. You may be tempted to shorten your breath, but keep your focus and breathe deeply and deliberately.

The power to concentrate the force is in the exhale. Weightlifters and bodybuilders will be familiar with this principle because they know when you are manipulating a physical object your power to move it is always greater upon exhale. Keep the same slow, even rhythm to your breathing as you would if you were lifting weights in the gym.

If you are unfamiliar with weight lifting, use the 6-3-6-3 rhythm of yogic power breathing. Those unfamiliar with this method will want to practice with breathing alone, at first, until they master the rhythm without having to actually count. To do this exercise, inhale for the count of six and hold for the count of three. Then, exhale for the count of six and hold for the count of three. Then, repeat this inhaling, holding, exhaling and holding rhythm over and over, again. Beginners should start with 10 to 15 repetitions at a time.

After you have collected and compressed the akashic energy ball for a few minutes, begin drawing in the element of fire. This is an energy, dense enough to appear as a white mist tinged with red. By the same method, draw it and compress it into the existing energy ball for a few minutes.

Add a little of the water element to the ball in the same manner as before. This is a white light tinged with a blue-green color. It swirls around in the air like a mist and has to be pulled into the ball. See it being sucked in like swirls of smoke being pulled into a vacuum. The fire and water element together intensify the electricity present in the akashic force, making it even denser and more active.

The air element occurs naturally between water and fire. You do not have to go out of your way to create it.

Further strengthen the energy of the ball by adding to it a little element of earth, which is dense, heavy-feeling, white light, tinged with yellow and reddish-brown. This brings the energy ball even closer to the physical level.

After you have done this, you should feel a tingling sensation. You may experience surges of energy all throughout your body that cause you to shake involuntarily or experience muscle spasms. If you are a crime survivor these sensations may be very familiar to you. The difference is, when you draw the energy in deliberately through meditation, the sense of malice and the desire to do harm is absent. You feel the purity of the force coursing through your body, shaking you from your core outward and causing your muscles to twitch, but without the usual rage attached to it.

Releasing the Force

Regardless of what method you use to generate and concentrate the etheric force, the technique of releasing it on a target is the same. Although, the traumatized crime survivor has some distinct advantages when it comes to honing in on the energetic pattern of the offending party. Fortunately, the art of spell casting, using sound magical theory, can provide other means for finding the target in cases where the magician is unable to use his or her mental power so directly.

The release of the force occurs naturally when the energy inside your body reaches the point of bursting because you can no longer contain it. It may be dispersed by forcing it out of the body at the navel or through the palms of the hands and through the finger tips. It may, also, effectively be released through the eyes, if you are looking directly at your subject or something that energetically represents him.

When you perform a spell, it is helpful to have an item that represents the person you wish to affect upon which to project this force. Such items include a photograph, hair or nail clippings, a spot of blood, clothing with bodily fluids on it or anything that belongs to the person, which they have carried with them that would be impregnated with their energetic signature. Although, it is not always possible to obtain such items, especially in cases where you are being targeted by criminals who have purposely hidden their identities.

In these instances, you must use your imagination a little more. If your oppressor is a company, you will have to consider the entire organization in your spells. If all you have to work with is the name of your enemy, then you must use this. But, make use of whatever information you can obtain.

You may, also, tap into the energetic signature of the subject entirely with your mind if your powers of concentration are great enough. This method is easily used by those who suffer from persistent, haunting memories of violence because they carry in their memories an irrepressible, usually perfect energetic imprint of their enemy. Any way that you can mentally tap into the energetic signature of your enemy provides you with a connection to him through which you can release the full impact of the etheric force.

Exercise 2

Once you have accumulated and condensed the etheric force, use your desire or your *will* to release the energy in whatever manner you choose. Energy released in a burst through the abdomen or the solar plexus produces a strong impact like a cannonball. When it is released through the eyes, it hits the target very precisely. The release is usually more controlled when it is done through the palms of the hands and the finger tips.

The instant you think it is going to be done, it is done. The more you do it, the more comfortable you become with how it feels when the energy hits the target.

If you practice striking enemies who are right in front of you and observable, you will know that your technique is working. Then, you will be more confident when you release it at a distance on a representative of the subject or by making contact mentally by means of an energetic signature.

The techniques used in black magic are very similar to those used in healing. Moreover, learning to heal increases a witch's knowledge base and power for any other purpose. It is the case in witchcraft worldwide that black magicians are among the most powerful healers. Although, they are usually sought out only as a last resort. A stunning example of this is the Aghori of India, who are practitioners of a destructive aspect of Hinduism. They dwell in cemeteries as their practice revolves around the spirits of death who have command over not only death, but rebirth, regeneration and rejuvenation. They are shunned and feared by the rest of society, but well-respected for their seemingly miraculous healing abilities.

If you want to learn how to harm someone at a distance with precision, then learn how to heal. The techniques for releasing and manipulating the energy accumulated in the first exercise are very similar to those used in healing. Although in healing, the energy is released very slowly and gently so as not to harm any of the organs of the body. In harming magic, the energy can either be released slowly or in a burst like a wrecking ball.

The book, *Magical Healing: How to Heal Yourself and Others with Your Mind*, by this author discusses how to manipulate this energy for healing purposes. But, information about how to harm is imbedded in this book, if you read between the lines. For example, damming up the flow of energy in a body can cause weakness, fatigue and eventually tumors in the glands. Rapidly over-energizing the heart can cause it to fail. Inflaming the brain with the element of fire propelled from a distance by means of your will can cause severe headaches.

Projecting the Etheric Force

Witches are well-known for being able to project themselves into other objects or animals. This may be done by going into a sleep-like trance and consciously releasing an aspect of the etheric body. But, this can, also, occur spontaneously.

If you are a violent crime survivor, you may have already experienced spontaneous etheric projection through dissociation. It may happen the first time or two that you are the victim of a surprise attack or sexual assault that your mind uncontrollably dissociates from your body.

This spontaneous etheric projection may occur in the context of disbelief, when the victim cannot believe that the present horror is actually being perpetrated on them or to save the victim from physical pain or psychological trauma that is too great to bear. It is characteristic of rape and especially violent attacks.

It is part of the practice of physical self-defense to learn how to stay in the body, stay conscious and, if possible, fight during such attacks. This has to be done by practice; the ability is acquired after you have been unexpectedly attacked a couple of times. You then begin to establish some control over this spontaneous dissociation.

To elaborate on the dissociation that occurs in the event of a terrible crime or even an accident involving the sense of being near death, an aspect of the astral body separates, so that the victim is viewing the event from the standpoint of a third-party observer. Some survivors describe floating over their bodies or simply being present while viewing the event from some other angle.

This is the experience you will be re-creating in the following exercise, but in a controlled way.

Exercise 3

Sit comfortably in a room where you can be alone and undisturbed. Focus your concentration on an object across the room such as the leg of a chair, a door knob or a plant. By means of your imagination, transfer your perspective so that you are now seeing the room from the point of view of that object. Allow your consciousness to remain in the object for a few seconds as you get used to the feeling before returning to your own physical perspective.

Practice doing this with various inanimate objects for a while until it becomes easy and natural to you.

Then, use the same technique on a bird you see perched outside your window or flying through the sky. Simply project your consciousness into that creature's body. This is largely an exercise of imagination, at least, in the beginning. After a while, you will begin to see things that do not seem to come only from your imagination.

You may use this ability to investigate your enemies, their activities, their associations and their locations. Once you have mastered this, you can do it while you are fully awake and engaged in other tasks.

Transferring Etheric Force from One Object to Another

It is a general principle in healing, particularly recognizable in the curanderismo (healing) aspect of Mexican witchcraft, that energy may be transferred from one living thing to another. This is the concept that lies at the heart of the Mexican Limpia, the cleansing ceremony performed by Mexican healers involving a chicken egg.

This principle of energy transference is, also, illustrated in the New Testament wherein the magician and exorcist, Jesus Christ, cast demons into the body of swine. Subsequently, the swine committed suicide by running over the edge of a cliff.

While this method is used primarily in healing and exorcism, it can be used in malefic witchcraft. Demonic entities and some illnesses can be transferred from one person to another by means of concentrated effort on the part of a trained magician.

It is possible to heal a friend or yourself while you harm an enemy by mentally transferring the affliction from one person to another.

Making Black Magic Spells Work

Black magic may have been the first form of witchcraft. The further back the history of witchcraft is traced the darker and more malefic it becomes. Modern witchcraft, particularly, popular witchcraft in the form of the religion Wicca, is very benevolent by contrast, which is why it is necessary to speak so frankly about the more traditional aspects of witchcraft. In more traditional cultures, this would not be necessary because the malefic aspects of witchcraft are very well known and those who practice it are feared.

Witchcraft has always been the domain of two main classes of people: (1) The highest echelon of the ruling class and (2) the most oppressed of the underclasses.

It is well known that ancient and medieval kings and even modern political leaders from Adolf Hitler to Ronald Reagan had ties to the occult. Their advisors included magicians, astrologers, psychics and demonologists.

In Western Europe the most oppressed underclass was women, especially single women and widows. In the United States, women were joined by the American Indians and African-Americans. Perhaps the most powerful magical system in the United States is American Hoodoo, which has its foundation in a variety of practices from different sources, including the American Indians, the Hebrew Kabbalah, Western Europe and Africa. The African spiritual roots of Hoodoo are especially primal and powerful because they were forged in ancient times, then steeped in the darkness of oppression and injustice in the United States.

African spiritualism has been subjected to ridicule by the popular media and to simply being swept under the carpet by most modern historians, which is where the wealthy, white, Christian, male power structure hopes it will remain because it is, in fact, so extremely powerful. This system tried very hard to destroy African spiritualism because they feared its power in the hands of those whom they had deeply wronged and, therefore, they sought to replace it with Christianity with its doctrines of forgiveness of evil, mildness, meekness and turning the other cheek.

Slavery continued in some American states for decades after the Civil War. During these years, American Hoodoo grew more powerful, incorporating concepts from a variety of other sources. It was around the time of the outbreak of the Civil War that researchers like Mary Alicia Owen began documenting these practices, although in many places, like New Orleans, practicing Hoodoo would remain illegal for many decades to come.

These old Hoodoo practitioners were faced with very much the same kinds of problems that are faced by the modern underclasses. There are still problems of harassment and oppression by the authorities and more affluent and powerful classes of people.

Furthermore, despite the perceived social openness present in modern culture, there are still crime-related subjects that are considered taboo. They are little talked about either because they are too horrible or because many people do not believe such crimes occur and for survivors breaking down those walls of disbelief seems impossible and useless. Even when crimes are acknowledged by society or the legal system, it seems that justice is something that only a select few can afford. Therefore, many old Hoodoo techniques are very applicable to modern life.

An investigation into witchcraft practices worldwide shows that the fundamental principles of black magic and spell craft, in general, are very similar. Fundamentally, they involve accumulating energy and sending it to a target. This is accomplished either directly or by means of sympathetic magic.

When using any of the spells in this book, gather your etheric energy, whether through meditation or through raw emotion as a crime survivor, then apply it to the items used in the spell or directly to your enemy by means of telepathy. Work with confidence and when the spell is finished, release the energy completely, like an archer releases an arrow from his bow.

CRIMES AGAINST PROPERTY

By definition, a crime is an act that deprives another person of life, liberty or property. Crimes against property consist of trespass upon, damage to or theft of your possessions in a number of different ways by a variety of different types of perpetrators.

Burglary is a common type of crime against property. Burglars are people who enter your home or business without your permission. If you are not there, they may only steal from you, however, if you are there, you may be both robbed and possibly injured or killed. Currently, almost every place in the country, even places once thought of as safe and serene, are under siege by such criminals who enter people's homes or businesses and take everything of value they can carry.

Even if you believe you live in a safe place, you

should always take ordinary precautions against burglars. Common sense says you should lock your doors, whether you are home or not, and install dead bolts and sturdy metal doors, which cannot be easily penetrated.

Sometimes an intrusion on your property comes when you least expect it. At other times, you know when you are at an increased likelihood of becoming a target. For instance, you might consider a break-in more likely and take extra precautions if unsavory characters moved into the neighborhood or if you learned a neighbor's house had been robbed.

If circumstances warrant it, take even more precautions. For example, you may want to make use of surveillance equipment, which can discourage criminals. If you cannot afford surveillance equipment, you can get authentic-looking fake cameras rather cheaply.

Alarms and alarm services may help discourage burglars. But, they can be expensive and involve contracts. The alarm companies will automatically place a 911 call on your behalf. This means the police will come and you may have problems with them, as well.

Fortunately, online stores and Ebay are good sources for both authentic-looking fake cameras and signs that resemble those from major alarm companies, which you can place in your yard. If you don't want to invest in an expensive alarm system but would like to be alerted at night, in case of a security breach, hardware stores sell small, inexpensive alarms for your windows and doors, which will make a loud noise, if they are rattled or disturbed.

Arm yourself as best you can. Learn the laws in

your city and state. If you can have a loaded gun, keep one handy. Use your discretion. If you live in a city or state with restrictive gun laws, you may have to weigh the costs of breaking the law against your need to defend yourself and your property from violent criminals. Your safety, the safety of your family and your basic right to self-defense should always be foremost in your thoughts.

If there have been thefts in your neighborhood, talk to your neighbors to determine the thieves' modus operandi. Ask questions like, "How did they enter the premises?" "What time of day or night did they do it?" and "What did they take?" Use this information and take precautions, accordingly.

If you have small valuables like jewelry or coins, put them in a safety deposit box. If you have guns or electronics, which are favorite items of thieves, keep them well-hidden. When thieves come into someone's house, they are usually in a hurry and they will grab whatever is within reach. Putting something in an unlikely place or out of reach will make it more difficult for them. If you own your own home, consider installing safes in the floors and walls, which cannot be easily detected.

These are all basic, common sense actions you can take in such circumstances. Once you have physically secured your property, you may begin magically protecting it.

Protection of the Archangels

One of the most powerful methods of protecting your house is to surround it with the presence of the archangels. This spell works by visualization and invocation.

The archangels are beings of light, whose

counterparts are the dark, deformed fallen angels or demons. Demons and possessed or obsessed people, including criminals, are terrified of them. They are very powerful beings of light who can, also, take on different forms. They can be terrifying-looking, which is in contrast to the more demure depictions of them in Christian art. It is their function to help you whenever you call upon them.

Begin by sitting quietly for a moment as you imagine the archangel Michael. Envision a being seven to eight-feet tall, clad in bright red and blue, radiating light, with long, silver hair who is armed with a long sword. He is both beautiful and absolutely terrifying. Hold this image in your mind for a minute or two as you solidify it.

Now, invoke the protection of the archangels. Say the following words aloud:

I call upon you, Michael, who once before defeated the army of darkness, to send your soldiers to surround and protect this house from all evil.

From now on, whenever you see your house, you will be aware of these tall, armed angelic sentinels encircling your dwelling, facing outward with their swords drawn, ready to do battle.

Now, call upon angels to protect the interior of your home. Say:

I call upon the protection of the archangels to secure my home from anyone with malicious intentions.

If any evil-doer tries to enter your home, he will get a big surprise. These beings are absolutely terrifying when they are interacting with dark forces. Their faces become horrible and distorted, although they maintain their light form. Any uninvited person who succeeds in getting through your doors or windows will immediately flee in terror upon seeing them.

For further protection, place a protective spell on all of your valuables.

To Call a Dragon to Guard Your Possessions

Traditionally, dragons are guardians of treasure within the earth. Call upon a dragon for protection with this spell. You may see your dragon as an ancient spirit you have called forth or as a thought-form of your own creation.

Close your eyes and see a huge, red, fire-breathing dragon in your mind's eye. When you have this image fixed in your mind with rich detail, say:

Ancient dragon, I summon thee from thy lair in the bowels of the earth.

Guard my possessions and send terror and confusion to my enemies!

Let thy wrath be dark and terrible against thieves and those with malicious intentions.

Allow no harm to come to my possessions, let all evil take flight!

No evil-doer shall come near, nor touch that which belongs to me. So be it!

Charge and refresh this image of the dragon guarding your possessions, at least, once per week, pouring etheric energy into it, each time seeing it become more vivid and powerful.

House Blessings

If you have access to a priest, pastor or other knowledgeable spiritual leader, ask him or her to bless your house. You do not have to share their faith to benefit from this. This is just another layer of protection.

You do not have to be Catholic to bless your house with Holy Water, either. Although, in the United States, you may have difficulty obtaining it year round. Some churches now only make Holy Water available at certain times during their liturgical calendar. Do not be afraid to call a local Catholic Church and ask if they have Holy Water available. They will probably be more than happy to let you have some. Frequently, it is kept in a decanter at the back of the church and you can just go in with a little bottle and collect it.

This water has a very high vibration. If you are sensitive, you can feel it. Sprinkle it around your house inside and out. You do not have to do another thing. But, you can add your own prayer or incantation to the process, if you like.

You can, also, bless your own water, oil or salt. A powerful procedure for blessing water and salt for either sprinkling or bathing, which is called *A Ritual Bath to Purge Negative Entities and Restore Peace of Mind,* is described in *Chapter 9.*

Anointing Oil

Anoint every opening in your house and bless it with anointing oil. Plain olive oil works well for this purpose. You may, also, use other pure oils like sesame, sunflower or almond. For added power, make your own special preparation by adding 5 drops of myrrh and 5 drops of frankincense to 2 ounces of oil.

Blessed Salt

Sea salt is a very powerful banishment tool. Hold some salt in your hand and say over it:

Being of earth. In the name of the Ineffable God and by the Power of the Tetragrammaton, be thou consecrated in the service of the Most High. Guard and protect this house and everything and everyone in it from all evil.

Sprinkle this blessed salt around your house or apartment, across all thresholds and around all window sills.

Crystal Protection

Bury protective crystals on your property at the four cardinal points. For this spell, choose four clear quartz pieces, which are large enough to fit into the palm of your hand.

Place the crystals in a solution of sea salt and water for, at least, five minutes to cleanse and clear them. Afterward, assemble them together in one place and hold your hands over them, palms down, to program them. Recite the following words:

By the power of N., I charge you to protect this house from evil and all enemies, to ward off all who approach with bad intentions and to allow only friends to enter here.

In this instance, "N." represents whatever powerful spirit you want to call upon to assist you.

Then, using a compass, find the four cardinal directions and bury one of these crystals at the edge of your property at each of those points. If you live in an apartment, place the crystals inside your house at these points.

Mexican House Protection Spell

Obtain a small aloe vera plant. Pull it out of the dirt and rinse its roots under water. Place a clove of garlic in the middle of it. Tie the root end with a red ribbon and hang it on the outside of your front door. The plant will stay alive and protect your house from all evil.

Place a string of garlic across your doorway to ward off evil spirits. If you cannot obtain a strand, hang a single bulb above your doorway.

Pentacle Protection

To protect from evil, trace the symbol of the pentacle with your finger upon each door and window on the inside of your home.

Begin with the left-most point, tracing it to the right and finally ending at the same point at which you began. From this point draw a circle in a clock-wise direction around the five-pointed star. Charge this image with the power of the etheric force.

You will not see the pentacle, but it's energetic imprint will be there protecting the openings of your home. Refresh and recharge the pentacle regularly.

Spells for Victims of Theft

If you have already become the victim of thieves, there are some ways to psychically identify them and make them return what they have stolen.

To Discover the Identity of a Thief

If you believe you know the name of the person or people who might have stolen from you, but are not absolutely certain, this spell will help you determine the true identity of the thief.

Write the names of each individual you suspect on a slip of paper and place them into a bowl of water. Swirl the bowl gently and say, "Thief reveal yourself." Whichever slips of paper rise to the top represent the thieves.

Alternatively, use a pendulum to discover the thief.

If you are not already familiar with the practice of pendulum dowsing, begin by establishing which of the pendulum's movements represent "Yes" and "No" for you. For most people, if the pendulum swings back and forth, this means "Yes" and if it swings from left to right, this means "No." But, it is not the same for everyone, so you must ask the pendulum to tell you what motions mean "Yes" and "No." Once you have established this, you can proceed.

If you think you know the names of the possible thieves, write each name on a paper. Hold the pendulum over each one and ask if this is the name of the thief. Wait for the pendulum to give the answer.

If you do not know the name of the thief, take a piece of plain paper, cut it into 24 little pieces and write a letter of the alphabet on each one. You can either turn them over or leave them face up. Then, take your pendulum and have it show you the initials of the thief. After you have his initials, you can proceed to determine his entire name the same way. Just put the pendulum over each letter and ask if this is correct. Always be very specific in your questions to the pendulum and wait until it gives you an answer before moving on to the next letter. This method takes patience and focus, but it works very well.

A Ouija or spirit board session can, also, be conducted to obtain the name of the thief. You can do this alone or with another person.

Spell to Make Thieves Return Property

Stand in the doorway through which you believe the thieves entered, take three steps backward into your house and with all the force you can muster say:

Thief, thief, return with the stolen article. You are compelled by All the Powers of the Universe. By the Power of All that is Holy, you shall enjoy no peace nor rest, but you shall be tormented until you return the things you have stolen to me, the rightful owner. You must run and leap, you cannot rest nor sleep until you return. The Powers of Heaven bind thee, the Powers of Earth compel thee and the soles of your feet blister and burn! You will die lest you return and bring back what you have stolen to this place.

As you say these words, visualize the thieves bringing back your stolen goods. See it in your mind. When you go to sleep this night, again, imagine your property being returned to you before you fall asleep.

Story About Identifying a Thief and Retrieving Stolen Property

One day, a thief stole a small, but expensive item from a metaphysical bookstore. The owner of the store psychically gathered as much information about the thief as possible, including the name and verified it as best she could. Then, she mentally repeated to herself, "N. will come back into the store and return my property."

That night, the store owner could not sleep. Thieves don't just steal physical objects, they steal your trust. This particular thief was only a young girl, but the store owner was so angry that she could not have any sympathy or kind feelings for her and so she conjured and commanded dark spirits to torment the girl until she returned the object.

The next day, a girl who looked very much like the thief from the day before came into the store. Upon seeing her, the store owner asked, "Is your name N.?"

The girl replied, "Yes."

So, the owner asked, "Where is my property?"

The girl looked confused. She didn't have the store's property. In fact, she had never been in the store before, she said.

Upon second glance, the store owner realized this was not the same girl, but one who looked very much like her and who had the exact same name. While she was explaining the whole thing to this girl and apologizing, a man brought the stolen property in and placed it on the counter. He said he was sorry that his niece had taken it and thanked the store owner for not prosecuting.

The store owner's conjuration was very effective in bringing a girl by the same name as the thief and returning the stolen merchandise because it was infused with self-righteous rage. You must concentrate a strong force within yourself to make any spell work. Simply going through the motions is not enough. You have to put all you've got into it.

You can place a spell or curse on your property in the event that it is damaged or stolen. Such spells are described in *Chapter 5. Police Brutality, Official Corruption and Theft During Travel*. You can, also, conjure spirits to return thieves, to torment them with spirits until they return your property and to punish them, as described in *Chapter 7. Problems at Your Workplace or School* with regard to conjuring demons to stop unwanted behaviors and obtain revenge.

Angela Kaelin

WHITE COLLAR THEFT AND BANKING FRAUD

Theft by bankers has become an increasing problem, especially, since the repeal of the Glass-Steagall Act and the massive bank bailouts. The vast scale of these crimes has not yet been revealed in its totality.

The bankers have run amok. Whenever they have been unable to re-write laws in their favor they simply ignore them. If you have a contract with a bank for a mortgage or a credit card, chances are they have violated their contract with you, if there was ever a valid contract to begin with. The amount of fraud involved in the mortgage industry is mind blowing. Some experts estimate that possibly 90% of mortgages issued in the past 15 to 20 years are illegitimate.[4]

This means, if you have a house with a

mortgage, it is likely no one has a legitimate claim on your house except you. In many instances, multiple banks have stepped forward in an attempt to foreclose on a house only to find that none of them had a claim. Some of this is happening because of the fraudulent sale of securitized loans to multiple buyers, which occurred a few years ago. In other words, the bankers defrauded each other by selling phony mortgage packages over and over again. So much for honor among thieves!

The biggest obstacle to bringing an end to all the fraud is the glamor spell the banks have over them, which makes them appear legitimate. It is all a deception. Theft by deception is still theft. Even if the thief is wearing a nice suit and works in a big, luxurious office building, he is still a thief.

So, the first defense against these fraudulent bankers is to understand the illusion. They are like "the man behind the curtain" in *The Wizard of Oz*. It is, also, important for us to get over the idea that they are an authority of any kind or worthy of respect.

Eventually, this banking fraud nightmare may run its course and the true nature of the banking institutions and the crimes they have committed will emerge into the light for all to see. Until the glamor spell is broken, it is probably wise to stay out of contracts with them.

If you are in danger of losing your house, do not give up without a fight. According to legal experts, most of the time, their paperwork is in disarray or simply non-existent. Moreover, the evil-doers purposely obscured their identities in these transactions to keep from being prosecuted at a later date because they knew they were defrauding the public. Therefore, trying to single out perpetrators in this mess is next to impossible.

On the physical level, it is important to do your research and consider the advice of legal and financial experts. *Default: Escaping the Debt Trap And Avoiding Bankruptcy,* by Heidi Guedel and *Clouded Titles: Who Really Owns Your Home?* by David Krieger are two examples of informative books on the subject of debt fraud.

Once you've done your research, begin working on the metaphysical level.

Spells to Stop White Collar Criminals Who Try to Steal Your Home or Your Money by Deception

For these spells, gather what information you have about whoever is persecuting you. If you have paperwork, a name, a phone number or an address, use that to bind the company and their minions. The idea is to have a point of mental and emotional focus so you can establish resonance with these criminals and have the effect you want on them and their environment.

While these crimes may be less intrusive than violent crimes or direct crimes to your property, such experiences can still be very traumatizing. Moreover, if you have suffered from more intrusive crimes in the past, such events as these can cause old memories of those horrors to resurface. Any trauma endows with you a measure of the gift of rage, which you can use to strike back at your enemies.

Santa Muerte Vengeance and Death Spell

Obtain an image of Santa Muerte, the Catholic folk saint who is the Spirit of Death in Mexico and an extremely powerful guardian who will be very aggressive with your enemies. She has enjoyed a resurgence in popularity in the past several years as official corruption in Mexico has intensified. You may find her at your local Mexican tienda, botanica, metaphysical store or online.

Santa Muerte is not recognized as a saint by the Catholic Church, but she is considered to be the mother of all. You can ask anything of her, including the violent destruction of your enemies, and she will grant your wish without judgment. She is very powerful, but she requires devotion. If you use this spell, give her a special place in your home with a devotional statue and she will help you with anything else you need.

You will need the following items:

Image of Santa Muerte in a black robe (statue or prayer card)
Black altar cloth
Black candle
Shot glass of tequila or whiskey
Document that represents your enemy
Small box or bag

Place the cloth on your altar, allowing it to drape slightly over the sides. Place the candle on your altar before the image of Santa Muerte along with the tequila or whiskey.

Choose an item that best represents your enemy as you understand him, either as a person or an institution. You may use a document that represents the enemy, a signature or a piece of paper with the enemy's name written on it, if you have this information. Place this item on the altar before Santa Muerte. If you are using a statue of Santa Muerte with a removable scythe, place the scythe on top of the document to represent her power over your enemy.

Light the candle.

Then, stand with your hands on the altar as you attain a meditative state and conjure the etheric force within you. Disperse this force into the altar and the items on it. Afterward, make the sign of the cross three times and recite the following prayer to Santa Muerte:

Prayer to Santa Muerte

O, Most Holy Death, please relieve me of all envy, poverty and hate. Enlighten my home with your holy presence. I ask that you break and destroy any curses that may have been placed upon me or my home. Bless me with love, prosperity and good health. Bless all those who live in my home with peace, protection and well-being. Santa Muerte, you are my protector. Shield me from my enemies great and small. Destroy those who would harm me or my house. Amen.

Then, in a commanding, forceful voice, recite *Psalm 94*. If you are not Christian, don't worry, neither were the alleged authors, who include David the Giant Slayer and his son King Solomon, who was a powerful pagan sorcerer. Whenever you recite a Psalm for a spell, say each syllable clearly aloud because each one contains power specific to a particular purpose.

Psalm 94: A Prayer for Vengeance

O God, to whom vengeance belongeth, show thyself.

Lift up thyself, thou judge of the earth: render a reward to the proud.

Lord, how long shall the wicked triumph?

How long shall they utter and speak hard things? And all the workers of iniquity boast themselves?

They break in pieces thy people, O Lord, and afflict thine heritage.

They slay the widow and the stranger, and murder the fatherless.

Yet they say, The Lord shall not see, neither shall the God of Jacob regard it.

Understand, ye brutish among the people: and ye fools, when will ye be wise?

He that planted the ear, shall he not hear? He that formed the eye, shall he not see?

He that chastiseth the heathen, shall not he correct? He that teacheth man knowledge, shall not he know?

The Lord knoweth the thoughts of man, that they are vanity.

Blessed is the man whom thou chastenest, O Lord, and teachest him out of thy law;

That thou mayest give him rest from the days of adversity, until the pit be digged for the wicked.

For the Lord will not cast off his people, neither will he forsake his inheritance.

But judgment shall return unto righteousness and all the upright in heart shall follow it.

Who will rise up for me against the evildoers? Or who will stand up for me against the workers of iniquity?

Unless the Lord had been my help, my soul had almost dwelt in silence.

When I said, My foot slippeth; thy mercy, O Lord, held me up.

In the multitude of my thoughts within me thy comforts delight my soul.

Shall the throne of iniquity have fellowship with thee, which frameth mischief by a law?

They gather themselves together against the soul of the righteous, and condemn the innocent blood.

But the Lord is my defense; and my God is the rock of my refuge.

And he shall bring upon them their own iniquity, and shall cut them off in their own wickedness; yea, the Lord our God shall cut them off.

Drip some of the candle wax onto the item that represents your enemy and say the following words:

O Most Holy Death, whose power in the Underworld and on Earth is infinite, I, your child am in need of your help. With all trust and confidence I ask that if my enemy continues to pursue me, he will be met with the most horrible death. I ask that you shall strike him down with the vengeance of your holy scythe and that all his minions and masters shall likewise be laid to waste.

Drip a little more wax on the item. Then, say in a loud, commanding voice:

I ask, Santa Muerte, that you execute great vengeance upon them with furious rebukes and that they shall know your almighty power when you lay your bony hand of vengeance upon them.

Drip a little more wax on it. Then, say:

No Kingdom or Principality of my enemies shall remain standing in this world or any other.
The Lord Rebuke them! Selah!
Santa Muerte destroy them!
They shall trouble me, nor anyone in my house, no longer.
They shall have no quarter. They shall be rent asunder.
They shall be cut down in agony. They shall know great pain and suffering,
And be rendered helpless and dead upon the altar of their own voracious greed,
Because of their evil acts against me.
So be it! Amen.

Make the sign of the cross three times.

If your enemy continues to pursue a case against you, to harass you, stalk you, intimidate you or, in any other way bother you, he will end up dead by means of magic as a result. This death may come in the form of a car crash, he may fall into the trap of his own schemes or he may become the victim of a random psychopath. You need never lay eyes on your persecutor or speak to him. You must only find resonance with him by means of mental energy, through the object you choose to represent him.

If many people focus their energy on corrupt organizations this way, they will soon end up dead institutions and the criminals who run them will end up in exile, in prison or endure a just and painful death.

When this candle has burned down, take the wax encrusted item that represents your enemy, place it in a small box or bag and bury it in a cemetery or at a crossroad far from your home or place of business. Do not tell anyone about having cast this spell.

Summoning the Intranquil Spirit

A damned soul known as the Intranquil Spirit may can be sent to haunt and torment a person until they modify their behavior toward you. Most commonly the Intranquil Spirit is summoned and dispatched to return wandering lovers. But, it can, also, be employed to attack any kind of enemy and can have the effect of simply being annoying or driving someone to suicide, depending on the conjurer's will.

The Intranquil Spirit is actually any one of the

many spirits who reside in Hell. Some are more helpful and easier to manage than others. If you find one who works well for you, ask for its name so it can be summoned directly whenever you require its services.

Many practitioners warn against summoning the Intranquil Spirit inside your own home. The spirits have been known to torment the magician instead of or along with the subject of the spell. For this reason, you may want to perform this summoning in a location outside your home. The grave site of a person known to have committed suicide or murder may be used. If you are concerned about being followed home by evil spirits, make a point of crossing over running water before returning home.

You will need the following items:

Black Candle
Item representing your enemy
Intranquility Oil
Crucifix or cross
Sea Salt
Rosemary oil
Lavender oil

If you wish to torment a particular person or agent of a company or other organization into compliance with your will, obtain an item that carries the subject's vibration, such as a photograph, signature, correspondence or a similar article.

Anoint the item and the candle with Intranquility Oil using the following formula from the book, *Traditional Witches' Formulary and Potion-making Guide: Recipes for Magical Oils, Powders and Other Potions*, by Sophia diGregorio.[5]

Intranquility Oil
Use to Summon the Intranquil Spirit

1/2 cup sunflower oil
5 drops coconut oil
3 drops lavender oil
2 drops violet oil or the tops of 2 or 3 blossoms
Pinch of black pepper
2 drops ginseng extract
3 drops allspice oil
Pinch of powdered knotweed
Pinch of stinging nettles

Light the candle and place the item representing your enemy beneath or beside it. It is customary to hold a crucifix in your right hand, but you may substitute a plain cross. Invoke the spirit with the following incantation:

O, Intranquil Spirit,
You that in Hell are wandering and will never reach Heaven,
Hear me, O, Hear me.
I command you to grasp the five senses of N.
Give him no peace, neither seated nor standing, waking nor sleeping.
Oppress and torment him with darkness and despair.
I conjure you, N.
Before the cross and God Almighty,
That you are to run until you die,
As the living run after the cross,
And the dead run after the light. Amen.

As the candle burns out, meditate on what should happen to the offender. If you want him to go mad and commit suicide, envision this. If you want him to be covered with festering boils, then let your imagination run wild with this idea. When the candle has burned out, bury the refuse from this spell at a location far away from your home. If you are already in the cemetery, this is an ideal place. Once you've done this, forget the whole affair as if it never happened and return home without looking back.

Afterward, prepare yourself a cleansing bath of sea salt and a few drops of lavender or rosemary oil and relax in it.

Hoodoo Binding Spell

If you are not desirous of the total destruction of your enemies, you may choose to do a binding spell to prevent them from doing further harm.

You will need the following items:

Cloth doll
Black candle
White sage (optional)
Personal effect or other item representing your enemy
New needle
Black thread
Several feet of black yarn

Obtain a little cloth doll. You may stitch one or purchase one at a hobby shop, usually very inexpensively.

Sweep the area around your altar or burn sage to dispel any energies that might interfere with your operation. Then, light a black candle.

Place whatever represents your enemy, for example, the person's name, company name or significant correspondence they have sent you, inside the head of the doll and stitch it up with the needle and thread.

Wrap the doll with a long strand of yarn as you repeat these words:

I bind you, so you can do no evil. I restrain you, so you can do no harm.

Continue repeating the words as you feel the etheric force growing within you. Allow it to disperse into the doll as you continue binding it. When the candle burns down completely, collect the candle and the doll and bury them at a crossroad.

Freezing Spell

Obtain an item that represents the person or organization working against you. Dampen it and place it in the freezer to dampen and freeze any further actions on their part.

Ashes Spell

Take the object that represents your enemy in your hand and say: *Here are my enemies.*

Then, light the object on fire and let it burn to ashes in a fireplace, a large cauldron or large coffee can and say: *Now, they are ashes.*

A Spell to Bring Their Crimes to Light

Use this spell to bring your oppressors to justice. It is best begun on a Sunday during a full moon.

You will need the following items:

White 7-day candle
Sandalwood
New mirror
7 white taper candles
Document related to your account or case
Piece of parchment or clean white paper and a pen

Gather any paperwork related to the bankers who are cheating you. Poke a few holes into the top of the 7-day candle and fill them with several drops of sandalwood oil. Then, place it on top of a mirror with the reflective side facing up. Arrange 7 white tapers around it.

Recite the following words:

N., you have hidden in the shadows and eluded justice for too long,

Now your crimes are being exposed and you will be brought to justice.

You cannot run, you cannot hide. There is no safe place for you.

Your luck has run out and you are trapped behind iron bars.

You shall pay for your crimes against the innocent.

Write this on a piece of parchment or paper, fold it and place it beneath the center candle. Light the candles and allow them to burn for an hour or so on seven consecutive days or until they burn out.

Snuff out the candles in between sessions instead of blowing them out.

Work to Break the Glamor Spell Woven by Corrupt Institutions

In your meditations, spells and invocations, please, work to unmask the illusion of these stealthy, well-dressed thieves and the grip this international criminal class presently has on the world, which is the root cause of most of the intolerance, hatred, worry, strife, hunger, death and war in the world.

Please, encourage your friends to do their own spells, prayers or petitions, regardless of their belief or lack thereof, to bring such criminals to justice, to expose their evil and stop them from harming more people.

Angela Kaelin

POLICE BRUTALITY, OFFICIAL CORRUPTION AND THEFT DURING TRAVEL

It used to be that you didn't have to worry about the police unless you were a criminal; now, it seems the police very often *are* the criminals. Many people in law enforcement jobs appear to believe they are above the law and, unfortunately, all too often they are, as they are rarely prosecuted for their crimes. Crimes committed by cops are called "police brutality" or "police misconduct." These are pretty terms for rape, robbery and murder by law enforcement officials.

According to an article entitled, *Police Are Twice As Likely To Sexually Assault You And Five Times As Likely To Murder You,* by former drug raid cop turned good guy Barry Cooper, the "FBI's Uniform Crime Reporting statistics, between

January 2010 and September 2010, [indicate] 31 cops per 100,000 committed homicide and 73 committed sexual assault. In comparison to 100,000 of the general population (this includes blacks, whites, Mexicans, gang members, etc.) only 5 citizens committed homicide and 29 committed sexual assaults."[6]

It is not unusual to be subjected to illegal stops on the highways by various law enforcement agencies in the guise of some kind of public safety or security, supposedly looking for illegal aliens or stopping drunk driving. Take special care when traveling in the area from any U.S. border and 100 miles inward, which the American Civil Liberties Union deems the "Constitution-free Zone," because of the inordinate number of abuses by law enforcement agencies taking place there every year.[7]

Then, there is the increasing problem of the ever-expanding TSA (Transportation and Security Administration), whose incidents of murder, rape and sexual assaults on the elderly, disabled, women and even toddlers along with their thefts of money, electronics and other items have been well-documented in the media and discussed in online blogs and forums. Agents of the U.S. Border Patrol and Customs have been found guilty of similar crimes. (See www.CheckPointUSA.org, for articles about such checkpoints and advice for dealing with them safely.)

Compared to all of this, the idea of a common crook robbing you at a rest stop seems a small threat – and it is. You are far more likely to be violently assaulted, raped, robbed, maimed or murdered by a uniformed criminal these days.

Many large city police departments are recruiting their members from gangs, either knowingly or unknowingly. This has been a well-documented problem in some cities. And, in some places you only have to look at them to know what they are involved in, especially, if you have psychic abilities.

Therefore, let us assume that you are a generally, law-abiding citizen simply trying to get along in life and that you conduct your personal and business affairs with integrity.

When you are dealing with a cop in a normal situation, like a traffic stop, in which you know you were driving over the speed limit, you probably will not have much of a problem. In these instances, most experts will tell you to simply be polite, don't say any more than you have to, never volunteer information, certainly don't argue (they are murdering people for asking questions these days), sign the little ticket and be on your way.

Of course, the best thing to do is not speed and try to make sure your car's lights are in good working order. But, what do you do when you are pulled over for no reason except for the policeman's own personal gratification?

Now, you have a big problem because the police officer is committing a crime and when they commit one crime, they usually plan to commit a few more before they are finished with you. In these instances, you will probably not be able to identify the cop. If he is wearing a name tag at all, it will probably be obscured.

Frequently, cops will remove identification before approaching you with criminal intent. They will, also, keep their vehicles parked back far enough to be off their dash cameras. If you are a woman or a racial or other minority in such a situation, you are likely in grave danger, especially at night and in remote locations.

Armchair experts will tell you not to pull over at all under such circumstances, however, reality is different. If a cop gets behind your car and turns the lights on, you have very little time in which to pull over and stop. If you do not stop almost immediately, you run the risk having your car rammed, being shot at or severely brutalized when you do finally stop.

Once stopped, you must give them your identification. If your correct home address is on your driver's license, your problems with this thug may not end here because now he knows where you live. An innocent woman was once forced to leave her nice apartment, her work and run for her life after such a fraudulent stop by a highway patrolman who admitted he had been stalking her.

On the mundane side of protecting yourself, consider investing in some kind of audio and video recording devices. Nowadays, there are companies selling relatively inexpensive recording devices you can hide in your car. You will want them to be discreet because if the officer believes he is being recorded, he might destroy your device and, possibly, cause you severe bodily harm afterward. In many instances, recording law enforcement officers has proven to be the only defense innocent people have had against police brutality.

Take caution with the laws in some places, which forbid citizens from recording police. Learn the laws in your area and try to obey them. Then, begin protecting yourself metaphysically.

Defending Yourself Spiritually from Evil in Uniform

On a metaphysical level, when you are in a situation where you are confronted with a law enforcement officer who wants to violate you in some way, you are almost always dealing with someone who is actually demonic or possessed by something demonic. If you are psychically tuned in you may even be able to see their true nature or the entities in or around the person.

One man, who possesses the psychic power of discernment, prayed the demonic entities controlling a law enforcement officer away. He was stopped by a cop who was being especially difficult for no reason. He recognized that the man was possessed and mentally recited a little prayer to remove the demonic influence. Suddenly, the cop's facial expression softened and he became pleasant before urging him to quickly be on his way. The influence of the man's prayer was short-lived, but it gave him a window of escape.

Interestingly, some possessed people know that they are under the influence of a demonic entity. Many of them are just fine with it and do not find it to be a problem at all. But, such people are unpredictable and potentially volatile.

Many such people are attracted to law enforcement jobs. So, if you find yourself in a bad situation with one of them, silently command the entity to depart or call upon a spirit to help you restrain it. Call upon "the Lord," angels, demons or any powerful spirit, such as St. Michael or Santa Muerte, with whom you have a relationship to remove the evil spirits from the law enforcement officers until you can get away. You may, also, say the words of St. Jude when confronted with dark forces: "The Lord rebukes you."

Illegal Searches and Seizures

Any good lawyer will probably tell you never to let law enforcement officers search your car without a warrant. Unfortunately, sometimes they will search you or your vehicle without either your permission or a warrant. While you have the right to refuse a warrantless search as well as illegal detainment and false arrest, if you do not willingly submit to them, you and your family might be subjected to violence. So, you will have to weigh each situation as it arises.

Illegal searches and seizures are becoming increasingly common. Airport personnel and border control agencies have been doing this for so long that nobody seems to question it.

From a practical standpoint, there is not much you can do to keep these prospective thieves out of your personal belongings in some instances. For now, in the U.S., you may be able to avoid the TSA by avoiding airports and public transportation. But, if you are faced with a situation where your suitcases are likely to be searched, use the kind that snap shut rather than the kind with zippers. Even if you lock them, zippers can be quickly and easily breached by simply wedging something in between the teeth. They can open the bag, steal items from it or, worse yet, plant illegal items and zip the bag back up without you knowing your suitcase was opened.

If you travel much, consider insuring your cell phones and other electronics that you must travel with. Do not travel with family heirlooms or anything that has sentimental value to you. If possible, permanently mark your belongings with your name or initials inside a compartment or elsewhere where it cannot easily be detected on the slim chance you are able to bring the thieves to justice through the court system.

Beware of airport personnel who photocopy any of your financial documents or credit cards. If these are confiscated or kept out of your sight for any length of time, immediately contact the companies involved and let them know there may have been a breach so they can look out for fraud and issue new account numbers to you.

These are practical things to consider when you travel, but there are metaphysical remedies, as well.

Psychic Attack on Unknown Abusers

By means of witchcraft, you can avenge yourself on people who violate or abuse you. The following story illustrates how to conduct a psychic attack on a person about whom you have little or no information:

One woman stopped flying back in the late 1990s after she was sexually assaulted, gang-style by airport workers of some kind in Detroit. She believed they were U.S. Customs officers, but she never knew their identities or their purpose in attacking her and plundering through her things without her consent or ability to observe what they were doing.

After filing a complaint against the organization (and being told that they had no culpability, obligation to obey the laws of the land or even adhere to the constraints of common human decency), contacting lawyers and the airline concerned, her only recourse for justice was to take revenge by means of witchcraft on the main thug who had abused her.

He was a man of no small physical proportions. Although, she did not know his name, she remembered his face and his voice as he held up ordinary items from her suitcase and asked her what they were. She remembered distinctly how he looked and sounded when he held up a book and asked, "What is this?" as if he had never seen a book before. And, she remembered very clearly how he looked and sounded when he bellowed at her to "Shut up" when she asked why they were doing this to her. He was the one who ordered five other very large people to take her against her will and sexually assault her in a private room, while he and another huge man rifled through her things like common bandits.

Lying in the darkness, unable to sleep for days and weeks after the assault, she held these very clear images in her mind with burning rage. She reached her hand out into the darkness and imagined with amazing realism that she held this man's beating heart in her hands. And, in her rage, she squeezed it until it stopped beating and he died, thus rendering him unable to victimize any other innocent women. She was several hundred miles away when she did this spell, so, she did not actually see him die with her physical eyes. And, since neither he nor any members of his uniformed gang were identified to her, she had no way of checking the obituaries to verify this. But, whenever she remembered this man and the terrible things he did, she had the satisfying sense that he was safely dead.

Every successful spell first involves finding

resonance with your target. If you don't know names, you have to get a clear energetic imprint of the perpetrators from their faces, their movements and their voices. Once you have resonance, you apply your rage to the perpetrator with full force.

If you are a crime survivor, then rage is a powerful means of striking at your enemy at any distance, even with very little information about him. The face, the voice, the smells and the other horrors you cannot forget forge an energetic link to the perpetrator, which you can use to strike at him. Keep your rage by you. Foster it. Nurture it, so it becomes a formidable weapon when you need power to do any working.

To Cast a Protective Spell Over Your Possessions

In preparation for travel, place a spell over your possessions so that if they are touched by people without your permission, the perpetrators will be subject to automatic retribution.

A woman who often traveled for business endured frequent official abuses. Because she had been repeatedly harassed, stalked and molested by uniformed agents to the point that it was impacting her both psychologically and financially by affecting her ability to work, her spells were very angry.

She placed a spell on her things so that any person who touched them would become poisoned and die. To do this, she simply made an incantation to this effect over her belongings and sealed it with a pentagram drawn in the air as a shield.

To place a protective spell on your possessions, conjure the etheric force within you and visualize it entering the items you plan to travel with. Then, make a pronouncement over them, such as:

Whomsoever lays hands on these objects, my possessions, without my permission or with malicious intentions, shall be forever cursed. Bad luck will follow him for the rest of his days. None of his ambitions will be realized. He shall not prosper. His fortune shall be ruined. From this point forward, all of the misery he has inflicted on others shall return to haunt him whether he is sleeping or awake. His life shall be cut short and he shall suffer torment now and in the hereafter. Let him be damned now and forever more! So be it! Amen.

Spell to Protect Your Belongings

Salt has similar properties to clear quartz crystal in that it will do what you program it to do. Take a handful of sea salt in your left hand and speak to it, as if you were addressing a person:

Protect my belongings from thieves and all evil-doers.

Sprinkle the salt into your suit case and close it.

Charm Against Theft

Place two pieces of red flannel or cotton together and stitch three sides with black thread. Fill the center with equal parts of myrrh, juniper berries and blessed thistle. Stich the fourth side closed. Then, tuck this bag into an obscure spot in your suitcase.

Protection for Travelers

Spells and amulets for the protection of travelers are a very old concept because centuries ago, people feared bandits and predators on the road. Today, apart from our means of conveyance, little seems to have changed.

For Safe Travel at Night

If you must travel after dark, alone at night reverently recite, Psalm 121 seven times before your departure, as follows:

I will lift up mine eyes unto the hills, from whence cometh my help. My help cometh from the Lord, which made heaven and earth. He will not suffer thy foot to be moved; he that keepeth thee will not slumber. Behold, he that keepeth Israel shall neither slumber nor sleep. The Lord is thy keeper: the Lord is thy shade upon thy right hand. The sun shall not smite thee by day, nor the moon by night. The Lord shall preserve thee from all evil; he shall preserve thy soul. The Lord shall preserve thy going out and thy coming in from this time forth, and even for evermore. Amen.

Stop Harassment Powder

Harassment can be a problem regardless of your means of transportation. But, it is especially bad for girls and women who must walk or take public transportation to work or school. Many women who travel any distance by car, also, endure a barrage of harassment. Moreover, harassment may occur anytime or place along your journey and even at your final destination.

Combine equal parts of the following ingredients, mix and pulverize them:

Tobacco ashes
Chili powder
Nutmeg
Cinnamon
Powdered newsprint

To stop street and general harassment during travel, place this mixture in a little cloth bag and carry it with you. To stop harassment in a certain place, sprinkle this powder around the area where harassment most often occurs. To stop harassment by a particular person, sprinkle this powder around or near the harasser or the place he typically occupies.

Becoming Invisible to Predators

If you tend to be the target of harassment and you must travel far on the highway alone consider donning a disguise. A woman conducted the following experiment years ago because she would frequently acquire highway harassers and stalkers en route from point A to point B in the course of her work. She discovered that if she put her long, blond hair under a short brown, boyish-looking wig, wore dark glasses and a baseball cap that she had no problems, whatsoever, with highway stalkers of any kind.

Physically changing your appearance in the most superficial ways can help you become "invisible," if you are a person whose appearance attracts unwanted attention and other rude behavior.

In the furtherance of this experiment, one day the woman went into a new gym dressed as her normal self. A woman clerk was gruff and very rude to her and insisted she had to leave identification at the desk before she would be allowed in. While she was working out, the men in the gym wanted to help her find weights and give her unsolicited work out tips.

The next day, the same woman went back to the same gym, wearing dark glasses and a short brown wig. The same clerk from the day before was extremely friendly and smilingly told her to go right on back to the dressing room. She did not demand to see her identification and the woman was able to go into the gym and enjoy her work out without being bothered by anyone. Changing her outward appearance made her feel as if she were invisible.

Not only can changing your physical appearance in this way profoundly alter the way people treat you, it can help restore a sense of power to you. When you conduct an experiment like this for yourself, it helps to reduce some of the subtle doubts that victims of frequent harassment experience. Girls and women who are frequent targets of harassment and other bad behavior from strangers often fear that they are somehow the cause of it, that they are doing something wrong. But, performing this experiment will show you that there is nothing wrong with you and it helps you deflect the blame that others may try to cast on you when you talk about your experiences.

Invisibility Spell

Whether you don a disguise or not, you can cast a spell to render yourself invisible. The underlying theory of the power of invisibility is as follows: In order for you to be perceived by the physical eye, you must reflect light waves. Therefore, if you cease to reflect waves, you will become invisible.

To block the light rays reflecting off your body, mentally create and surround yourself with a cloud.

To do this, visualize a gray-blue cloud surrounding you and deflecting the light waves that would make you visible to others. Their eyes will pass over you as if you are not there. You are no longer reflecting light waves because they are hitting the inside of the cloud you are projecting and bouncing back to you.

Another way to do this is to obtain a clear quartz crystal. Cleanse and clear it. Then, program it to generate this cloud for you. Hold it in your hand and see a blue-gray cloud emanating all round the crystal and enveloping you, rendering you invisible. Refresh this spell every day by re-programming the crystal and envisioning this cloud emanating from it, shielding you from the view of others.

Over time, you will learn to mentally control the cloud. It will become more vivid and stronger, thus, providing greater, more reliable protection.

If you apply this spell while traveling in a car, do not use it to surround your entire vehicle, just yourself. The reason for this is that if your entire car becomes invisible, other drivers will not see you and you could become involved in an accident. You want to make only yourself invisible, so you are not a target of police and other highway stalkers.

Bloodstone Talisman for Invisibility

The bloodstone is so named because of what appears like flecks of blood in it. It is a very powerful healing stone; the energy it emanates is very near the physical plane. An older name for this stone is "heliotrope." "Helio" means sun and "trope" means "to turn." It was so named because of its powers over light rays. For this purpose, the stone is placed in water on a sunny day to turn the rays of the sun and bring rain.

This power of the bloodstone is, also, employed to turn the light rays produced by the physical body to render the magician invisible to others.

One of the most famous bloodstone invisibility amulets in history was carried by Brigham Young, the second President and prophet of the Church of Jesus Christ of Latter-day Saints (The Mormons), which is an organization with deep roots in witchcraft and the occult, although it is ostensibly Christian. Young's bloodstone, which he wore on a chain close to his skin when he went into any new or dangerous situations, is presently on display at the Pioneer Memorial Museum in Salt Lake City, Utah.

To program a bloodstone as an invisibility talisman, hold it between both of your palms and speak to the spirit of the stone, as follows:

O Holy stone, I command you to turn the rays that emanate from my body, so that when I will it, I radiate no perceptible energy waves and I am thus rendered invisible. So be it. Amen.

San Ramón Nonnato for Invisibility

San Ramón Nonnato (Saint Raymond Nonnatus) is a Catholic saint of 13th century Spain who is popular in Mexican witchcraft. Officially, he is the patron saint and protector of pregnant women and he helps priests keep the secrets of their confessors. But, he is, also, employed to keep secrets and hide people and things. His feast day is August 31st.

Call upon San Ramón to render yourself, your automobile, your home, your business and your possessions invisible.

Obtain a San Ramón prayer card and light a red candle before it, at least, once per week to establish and maintain a connection to him. Additionally, offer him a shot glass of whiskey. Recite the prayer to San Ramón on the back of the prayer card and petition him to protect you, your automobile and whatever else you wish to render invisible.

Keep a San Ramón prayer card with you when you travel and whenever you approach a checkpoint, touch the card and say, "San Ramón, cover me," so that you will be overlooked by law enforcement agents.

Power Over Machines

It is possible to affect mechanical and electrical objects with your mind. If someone harasses you on the highway, their car's engine over-heats and they quickly find themselves sitting along the roadside with steam rolling out. This is an amazing thing to see and it is a great relief when your harasser is almost instantaneously rendered powerless from doing you harm. You do it all with your mind by focusing and sending out your rage to the offending party and their vehicle.

Increasingly, highway harassment and, in particular, road rage has become a problem, often with deadly results for the victim. If you are being targeted and harassed on the road by another driver for whatever reason, get angry about it! Take your focused rage and project it at the vehicle. Strongly visualize the engine going up in flames. In a matter of seconds, the driver will not be troubling you any longer because he will be dealing with the problem of copious amounts of black smoke rolling out of the hood of his vehicle.

It's that simple. You just have to conjure your anger. Do not get scared. Never allow fear to dominate you because it will freeze your ability to do magical workings and empower the dark forces that dominate the evil-doers.

Just, get angry and focus your rage at your persecutor's motor.

A Mexican Charm for Safe Travel

Protect yourself and your vehicle during travel with a simple charm. The following story illustrates how such a charm may be used:

A couple made a trip by car from the U.S. to Mexico to visit their parents. To protect them on their way back home, the man's mother, who is a very powerful spiritual and herbal healer, tied a little bag of herbs under the seat of their vehicle so they would not meet with any harm on the way home. It worked beautifully. They never had so little trouble crossing back into the U.S., despite having to pass through several checkpoints within the two countries. They arrived home safely without encountering any difficulties of any kind.

To protect yourself and your vehicle from evil, obtain a cotton bag about 3" by 5" and fill it with equal parts of corn, rice and holy basil. Tie it up with a string. Then, place your hands, palms downward over this charm and recite an incantation over it, as follows:

Protect this vehicle and those who travel in it. Let them arrive safely to their destination. Let this vehicle and its passengers pass through all checkpoints without difficulty or harm. Keep them safe from accidents and evil. So be it!

Tie the bag to the inside of your vehicle, under the seat or somewhere where it cannot be seen.

Overall Protection for Your Vehicle

Take a picture of your vehicle and place it on your altar beneath a white candle. Sprinkle the photograph with a pinch of each of the following three herbs: Blessed thistle, yarrow and juniper.

Each one of these herbs imparts certain vibrations upon your vehicle by means of its image and works at a distance to protect it. Blessed thistle is for protection of the vehicle from theft and accidents, yarrow is for protection from evil influences and juniper is for the protection of your vehicle's contents.

Light the candle and sprinkle salt around the image. Then, recite the following incantation:

O Most High and Holy, send your guardians to protect my vehicle that it and all it conveys shall be safe from all evil whether accidental or malicious. Bless this vehicle and keep all who ride in it safe from harm. So be it!

Reinforce this spell once or twice a week by lighting a white candle and repeating the incantation.

Angela Kaelin

PROTECTION FOR YOUR HOME AND BUSINESS

As previously stated, a crime is an act that deprives another person of life, liberty or property. But, in the U.S. today, the definition of crime has been greatly expanded and the number of laws and ordinances are so great that even law enforcement agents and judges seem to be confused about what they are supposed to be doing.

As a result, in some places it is difficult to go about your legitimate business and live an honest life without interference from law enforcement agencies. Common targets of law enforcement intrusions include night clubs, farms and co-ops that grow and sell organic and raw foods, homeschoolers and legal medicinal marijuana dispensaries.

Your home or business may be invaded by SWAT-style police units who will abuse you, your family and your staff without benefit of warrants or any justifiable cause. Frequently, they are working "undercover," so they hide behind masks and you are unable to learn their identity, even in court. In cities like Houston, Texas, where raids on licensed businesses are common, owners and staff have difficulty telling the difference between a raid by armed, masked bandits and "legitimate" police raids.

ICE (U.S. Immigration Department) raids are a problem in some places, as well. These people can be extremely unpleasant and will think nothing of violating your rights. Yes, even if you are a citizen. A sizable number of those harassed, falsely detained or arrested in such raids are U.S. citizens who may be held without due process. U.S. citizens have even been falsely deported to foreign countries.

Brutal and unwarranted police interference has a profoundly negative impact on the rest of the survivors' lives. Many licensed, legal businesses live under the threat of these attacks every day, which is very stressful and traumatizing to the people in such circumstances.

The purpose of the following spells is to enable you to conduct your business and your personal life without interference from any kind of law enforcement agents. Among them are certain types of spells called Law Keep Away Spells. In Spanish they are called Contra la Ley (To Ward Off the Police). There are many such old spells for keeping law enforcement agencies out of your house or your place of business, especially in American Hoodoo and Mexican witchcraft.

Spells to Protect Your Home and Business from Intrusions

The I.N.S. (the old name for the Immigration Department) raided a company back in the late 1990s. It seems this raid may have been done entirely for the harassment of the business. They came under the pretense of looking for undocumented workers. Of course, they didn't find any, but they spent plenty of time illegally harassing and falsely detaining about 30 or 40 U.S. citizens. This company and its staff went through a period of time where they were inundated with undercover cops of some kind. No one knew why this was happening. After this particular raid, one of the employees at the company made a practice of anointing and burning a "Contra la Ley" candle at work, for protection from law enforcement agencies.

One day, this employee was told that some men from the FBI wanted to see her. They were in plain clothes and did not identify themselves. They began interrogating her about something she knew nothing about. Because she was unable to answer their questions, one of the men became angry and slid his arm around her neck and began strangling her. She broke free from his grasp and to attract attention to the situation, she began shouting as loudly as she could, "Dirty f--king cops! Right here! Everybody! Look at these dirty f--king cops!"

Her rage and the fact that she had outed these undercover officers to a group of onlookers drove them away as if the devil were chasing them. They ducked their heads, hid their faces and ran out of the place with their tails between their legs. Criminals and undercover cops don't like to be called out in public.

Prior to this strange visit, she had experienced several random attempts on her life by complete strangers, including a bizarre incident one night in which a man tried several times to run her down in the parking lot in front of her apartment.

To this day, she has no idea what this was all about. Possibly it was a case of mistaken identity since she is a very quiet, low-key, work-oriented personality and there is no cause for her having been the target of undercover police. Although, she couldn't help but notice that people around her were disappearing. Her colleagues believed one of their co-workers had been murdered and there was a general atmosphere of fear regarding law enforcement agencies because of past abuses.

She believes that her psychic awareness and her Contra la Ley spells kept her alive and warded off any serious attacks by law enforcement agents. These were strange times in this place, which will remain unnamed, but is now widely recognized as a dangerous border city. It is dangerous because of the many law enforcement agencies there who seem to be involved in some dark game that the rest of us know nothing about.

Contra la Ley or Law Keep Away Spell

Obtain a Contra la Ley 7-day candle, which are available from many metaphysical stores, botanicas and online stores.

Poke a few holes in the top of the candle and pour several drops of Contra la Ley Oil into them. The formula below is from the book, *Traditional Witches' Formulary and Potion-making Guide:*

Recipes for Magical Oils, Powders and Other Potions, by Sophia diGregorio.[8]

Contra la Ley Oil
Law Stay Away Oil

8 oz. almond oil
1 tsp. espanta policia (available from botanicas in the U.S. Southwest and Mexico)
2 tsp. fennel
1 tsp. anise
1 tsp. dragon's blood resin
1 tsp. licorice root
1 tsp. deer horn powder
1 tsp. Vitamin E oil as a preservative

Combine powdered, dry ingredients with the oils in a lidded jar. Set it in a warm place out of direct sunlight for two weeks. Strain the liquid through cheesecloth and bottle it. Afterward, store this potion in a cool, dark place.

After your Contra la Ley candle is dressed, write out a petition for protection on a piece of clean, white paper or parchment. State your intention clearly. If you only say, "Protect us from law enforcement," you may be protected from being seriously injured by them, but still get a nasty visitation, as this lady in the above story did. Do not make this mistake.

So, you should state your intention specifically. For example:

Do not allow any law enforcement personnel to enter this building for any purpose. Let them all be barred and restrained from entering. Render this building and all those who work here invisible to their sight.

Declare your will with the idea of barring the entry of all law enforcement agents, not just city police or Feds. Be specific according to your own situation. Burn your your candles in a place where they are safe and can be carefully watched during business hours.

Use a Contra la Ley spells to keep them away from your home, too.

You may use a Contra la Ley candle at your home for the same purpose. If you live in a house that is subject to false raids, this same candle spell can be helpful. This can happen, especially if you rent a house that was once the residence of a sought after person.

A woman once rented a house where twice cops came onto the front porch at five o'clock in the morning and shined a bright light through her bedroom window. This is a completely terrifying experience. They left when they realized the person they were looking for no longer lived there, but you never know what they might do in these situations and sometimes innocent people are injured and deeply traumatized. After the second visit, she began doing Contra la Ley spells and the visitations stopped.

To Open Your Third Eye
So You Can Recognize Danger

Sandalwood oil is regarded as a protective agent. It works by opening your third eye so you can see things coming and take action to protect yourself. Daily, anoint your third eye (at the center of your forehead) with sandalwood oil to further develop this kind of vision.

The bad part about this is you will be able to see things others cannot see and you will probably have difficulty warning them. But, at least, you will know what is happening. Don't waste any time in learning to trust your developing psychic powers.

If you see something unpleasant coming your way, ask for spiritual guidance to know how to handle the situation.

Old Bootleggers' Law Keep Away Spell

Another Law Keep Away spell comes from the Lucky Mojo web site (www.luckymojo.com). According to correspondence posted in the site's archives, there is an old spell that dates from the time of the bootleggers in the U.S. and is used to keep any kind of government agency out of your business.

It requires 4 copper pennies (preferably the old Indian Head kind) and 8 iron nails. The four pennies are arranged, heads up, in the formation of a cross upon the threshold of the main entry to your business. Each penny is held in place by two iron nails hammered in place on either side of the penny and folded over the top to form an "X" over each one. This keeps the bad guys from "crossing" your threshold and the heads up act as guardians.[9]

Devil's Shoestring Protection

Place nine pieces of devil's shoestring herb in a red cotton bag and carry it inside your clothes for protection. This will cause the government devils to become entangled, lost and unable to find their way to your home or business.

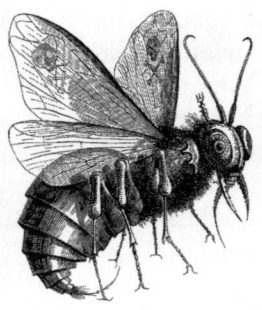

Flies and Cobwebs Spell

The following spell works very well to put a halt to incidents involving police harassment. You may need to rework it, at least, once a year if you live in a place where police harassment at your home or business is common.

Obtain a plastic baggie. A plastic zip-lock sandwich type will do very well. Go to your basement, your garage, barn or garden and collect as much spider web as you can find and put it in the bag. When you have done this go and find all the dead flies you can. Each one of these represents a cop. Place them one by one into the baggie with the cobwebs. Once you have collected as many "cops" as you can find to bury in the spider's web, seal your baggie and hide it somewhere in your home or business where it won't be found and forget about it.

Hot Foot Style Spell to Keep Government Agencies Away

To drive government persecutors away, on little strips of white paper or parchment, write the names of each and every agency that is plaguing you or your business.

Fill a pint or quart jar with a little vinegar. Add some black pepper, red pepper, horseradish and garlic powder. Add some dirt scraped from a grave (preferably that of a murderer) and powdered bones (bone meal). Use your creativity. Fill the jar with every nasty and repellent thing you can think of that might banish unwanted entities. Add some rusty nails or needles. When your imagination is exhausted, add the slips of paper, shake up the mixture and place the jar out of sight.

Court Cases and Legal Entanglements

Despite your best efforts to keep law enforcement out of your life, through no fault of your own, you can find yourself involved in a court case. Such occasions include false arrest, divorce, custody battles, visits from Child Protection Services and frivolous law suits.

In any case you find yourself involved in, the most important person you will want to gain mental influence over is the judge. In cases where there are witnesses or juries involved, you should include them in your spell work, also. Workings to influence courts are called "Justice" or "Court Case" spells.

Place a piece of Low John root (also known as galangal or court case root) into a red cotton or felt bag and keep it close to your body to gain influence over court proceedings.

Santeria for Success in Court

In any spell you use, you can incorporate a 7-day candle, prayer card, images and petitions to the following saints commonly used in Santeria spells:

St. James the Greater (Santiage Matamoros) is the patron of the plaintiff.

St. Cyprian (San Cipriano) is the patron saint of the defendant.

St. Lucy if you are an innocent defendant and you want your innocence to be seen in court.

St. Nicholas and Our Lady of Guadalupe or The Virgin of San Juan de los Lagos if children are involved.

St. Thomas Aquinas to help you and your lawyer see things from a different angle and find new strategies.

St. Anthony to improve your lawyer's performance in court.

St. Cajetan (St. Cayetano) and St. Anthony to help find evidence in your favor.

St. Jude and St. Rita for seemingly impossible or hopeless cases.

St. Dymphna to overcome stress and help you keep a clear head under pressure.

St. Expedite (San Expedito) to expedite proceedings when they are stalling.

Just Judge (Justo Juez) for absolute justice.

Honey Pot Spell for Court Cases

To gain the favor of a judge, jurors or other influential people involved in your court case or other legal matter, perform the following spell.

You will need the following items:

Short jar with a lid
2 pieces of parchment or white paper and a pen
Blue or brown candle or a 7-day candle
Honey, corn syrup or pancake syrup
Low John root (galangal)
Just Judge Powder (formula below)
Just Judge Oil (formula below)

Obtain a jar with a lid, place a piece of Low John root inside it, then fill it 2/3 full with honey or syrup.

On one of the pieces of parchment, write each of the names of the people you want to influence in your favor nine times in a column. Then, turn the paper 90 degrees and write your own name over the top nine times or as many as it takes to cover over the first set of names. If you are involved in a child custody case and you want the best outcome for the children, write their names over the top, instead.

Now, think for a moment about the ideal outcome in this situation. Then, write your request accordingly around the names in a circle, completely surrounding them, without lifting your pen. You may address your request to any deity, saint or other spirits you want to help you.

Dip the edges of both of the papers in Just Judge Oil and sprinkle Just Judge Powder onto the middle of the paper with the names on it. Then, place the blank sheet on top with the herbs in the middle and fold the papers toward you as if they were one, stating your desired outcome aloud as you do so.

Place the folded papers into the jar, submerging them in the honey or syrup.

Dress the candle with Just Judge Oil. Place it securely on top of the jar. Pour a little warm wax or a dab of glue on the surface of the lid to help keep the candle from slipping off. Sprinkle Just Judge Powder around it.

If you are in a hurry, this spell can be performed in one day or it can be drawn out over a period of several days or weeks by repeatedly speaking your petition and then burning the candle for about an hour and snuffing it out each day up until your court date.

Note: Put this jar and candle in a safe place so that if it falls it won't cause a fire.

Just Judge Powder

Mix and pulverize equal parts of the following herbs in a coffee grinder or a mortar and pestle.

Low John root
Carnation petals
Marigold petals
Anise seed
Cinnamon
Rosemary

Just Judge Oil

8 oz. almond oil
Add 3 pieces of Low John root or 8 to 10 drops Low John oil
8 to 10 carnation petals
5 drops marigold oil (or the petals of one or two flowers)
5 drops anise oil
5 drops cinnamon oil
5 drops rosemary oil

To Gain Influence Over The Court

Recite *Psalm 35*, A Prayer for Rescue from Enemies, aloud with passionate feeling:

Plead my cause, O Lord, with them that strive with me; fight against them that fight against me.

Take hold of shield and buckler, and stand up for mine help.

Draw out, also, the spear, and stop the way against them that persecute me; say unto my soul, I am thy salvation.

Let them be confounded and put to shame that seek after my soul; let them be turned back and brought to confusion that devise my hurt.

Let them be as chaff before the wind; and let the angel of the Lord chase them.

Let their way be dark and slippery; and let the angel of the Lord persecute them.

For without cause have they hid for her their net in a pit, which without cause they have digged for my soul.

Let destruction come upon him at unawares; and let his net that he hath hid catch himself; into that very destruction let him fall.

And my soul shall be joyful in the Lord; it shall rejoice in his salvation.

All my bones shall say, Lord, who is like unto thee, which deliverest the poor from him that is too strong for him,

Yea, the poor and the needy from him that spoileth him?

False witnesses did rise up; they laid to my charge things that I knew not.

They rewarded me evil for good to the spoiling of my soul.

But as for me, when they were sick, my clothing was sackcloth;

I humbled my soul with fasting; and my prayer returned into mine own bosom.

I behaved myself as though he had been my friend or brother;

I bowed down heavily, as one that mourneth for his mother.

But in mine adversity they rejoiced, and gathered themselves together;

Yea, the abjects gathered themselves together against me,

And I knew it not; they did tear me, and ceased not; with hypocritical mockers in feasts, they gnashed upon me with their teeth.

Lord, how long wilt thou look on?

Rescue my soul from their destructions, my darling from the lions.

I will give thee thanks in the great congregation; I will praise thee among much people.

Let not them that are mine enemies wrongfully rejoice over me; neither let them wink with the eye that hate me without a cause. For they speak not peace; but they devise deceitful matters against them that are quiet in the land.

Yea, they opened their mouth wide against me, and said, Aha, aha, our eye hath seen it.

This thou hast seen, O Lord; keep not silence; O Lord, be not far from me. Stir up thyself, and awake to my judgment, even unto my cause, my God and my Lord.

Judge me, O Lord my God, according to thy righteousness; and let them not rejoice over me. Let them not say in their hearts, Ah, so would we have it; let them not say, We have swallowed him up.

Let them be ashamed and brought to confusion together that rejoice at mine hurt; let them be clothed with shame *and dishonor that magnify themselves against me. Let them shout for joy, and be glad, that favor my righteous cause; yea, let them say continually,*

Let the Lord be magnified, which hath pleasure in the prosperity of his servant.

And my tongue shall speak of thy righteousness and of thy praise all the day long.

If you are called to testify or give a deposition, carry a little deer's tongue herb with you to impart eloquence to your words and help you communicate clearly and without misunderstanding.

If you are guilty, wear bergamot oil to gain mercy and forgiveness.

If you want to stop slander and false accusations against you, carry a little slippery elm in a cloth bag on your person.

Boost your Court Case spells by taking a bath with 9 drops of Just Judge Oil added to the water on the night before you must appear in court.

Hoodoo Spell to Win the Favor of a Magistrate

The following spell is from *The New Revised 6th & 7th Books of Moses and the Magical Uses of the Psalms*, originally published in Stuttgart, Germany under another title in 1849:

If you have business to transact with your magistrates or with your princes, and desire to obtain their special favor, then pray this Psalm [Psalm 5] early at the rising of the Sun and in the evening at sunset. Do this three times over pure olive oil, while at the same time you think unceasingly, upon the holy name of Chananjah (merciful God), anoint your face, hands and feet with the oil and say:Be merciful unto me, for the sake of thy great, adorable and holy name, Chananjah, turn the heart of my prince to me, and grant that he may regard me with gracious eyes, and let me find favor and courtesy with him. Amen! — — Selah! — — [10]

Recite *Psalm 5* three times over pure olive oil as follows:

Give ear to my words, O Lord, consider my meditation.

Hearken unto the voice of my cry, my King and my God; for unto thee will I pray.

My voice shalt thou hear in the morning, O Lord; in the morning will I direct my prayer unto thee, and will look up.

For thou art not a God that hath pleasure in wickedness; neither shall evil dwell with thee.

The foolish shall not stand in thy sight; thou hatest all workers of iniquity.

Thou shalt destroy them that speak leasing; the Lord will abhor the bloody and deceitful man.

But as for me, I will come into thy house in the multitude of thy mercy; and in thy fear will I worship toward thy holy temple.

Lead me, O Lord, in thy righteousness because of mine enemies; make thy way straight before my face.

For there is no faithfulness in their mouth; their inward part is very wickedness; their throat is an open sepulchre; they flatter with their tongue.

Destroy thou them, O God; let them fall by their own counsels; cast them out in the multitude of their transgressions; for they have rebelled against thee.

But let all those that put their trust in thee rejoice; let them ever shout for joy, because thou defendest them; let them, also, that love thy name be joyful in thee.

For thou, Lord, wilt bless the righteous; with favour wilt thou compass him as with a shield.

The Beef Tongue Spell

If someone is to bear witness against you, is slandering you or if you are involved in a law suit, the classic Beef Tongue Spell is intended to confound and silence your enemy.

You will need the following items:

Brown candle
A beef tongue from your butcher
Clean piece of paper
9 needles
Hot peppers
Slippery elm (optional, use it if you want to stop slander and false accusations)

Light the candle while saying:

N., you will come under my command. You will do as I say and hold your tongue.

Write the name of your adversary on the paper. Slice the tongue and stuff the paper and some hot peppers inside. If you are concerned about being falsely accused, put a little slippery elm inside, too.

Then, use the nine needles to close up the slit. Wrap the tongue up and place it in your freezer to cause your enemy to become tongue-tied and freeze up in court, thus rendering him unable to effectively speak against you.

The Creative Writing Spell

This spell works upon the basic principle of spell casting, which involves willing, finding resonance with your subject and fully releasing energy to allow it do to its work.

The following story illustrates this principle:

A teenager wrote down each of the things she wanted to do in life on about a dozen index cards and put them in a little box. She forgot all about them until a few years later when she and her grandmother were cleaning out a closet and found them. As she looked through each one of the cards, she saw that the things she had written on them had happened.

If you want something to happen, imagine it in the most vivid detail, write it down, then put it away and forget it for a while. For instance, if you want to see a robber, a rapist, a kidnapper, a killer, a corrupt cop, a wicked judge or any other villain brought to justice in some way or seek revenge on them for the wrongs done to you or your family, write this desire on a piece of paper, fold it up and put it in a box in the closet or in the bottom of an old drawer where it won't be found again for a very long time. When you come back to it, again, some day, you will see that it has come to pass.

If you have creative writing abilities, you can do this even more powerfully by writing a story in which your enemies are fictional villains who suffer explicit consequences for their evil actions against you according to your desires. In this story, accurately depict the events and distress of your real life experience using fictional characters who resemble yourself and other people important to your situation, concluding it with your desired outcome.

The following story illustrates the power of creative writing to affect the outcome of events:

A few years ago, an honest businessman became the victim of a corrupt judge after he was subjected to one of those terrifying, SWAT-style raids described at the beginning of this chapter. The court case was settled on a plea deal, he was not permitted a trial by jury and was given no opportunity to face his accusers who were unidentified undercover cops.

As a way to heal and purge her emotions about what had happened, his wife wrote a short story about justice coming to a fictional corrupt judge. Within a year or so, the judge in the original case was arrested for attempting to sexually coerce a woman who had been arrested (probably on false charges, as well). This brave woman blew the whistle and a corrupt judge was brought to justice, imprisoned and forbidden from sitting as a judge ever again. It didn't work out exactly like the fictional story the wife wrote, but this judge would never, again, be in the position to destroy the lives of more innocent people through the court system.

Interestingly, the novelist known as The Marquis DeSade, wrote shockingly vengeful tales about corrupt judges, such as *The Mystified Magistrate*, after being falsely imprisoned and mistreated by the courts in pre-revolutionary France. Perhaps, his work played a metaphysical role in the French Revolution.

There is a frightful feeling of power in being able to conjure visions of your desired outcome in a complex, personal conflict. Once you have written your story and given it the ending you desire, put it away and forget about it for a while. This is a way of releasing the energy of your will into the universe where it can begin working to produce the desired effect.

Bringing Justice to the World, Banishing the Evil-doers and Healing Our Nations

Maybe you know a law enforcement officer (including TSA, Customs, Border Patrol, etc.) or one is a member of your family. Even if they seem like good people, they are serving an evil master. Some of them are decent people in other areas of their lives, however, they are willing participants in crimes against citizens and, indeed, humanity.

If you know any of these people, shun them. Do not socialize with them. Do not invite them to your family dinner. This method is known to be highly effective among members of religious organizations like the Mormons, which is why it is used. It works by shaming the person. If they realize that what they are doing is socially unacceptable, they may stop serving the wicked, destructive forces that seek to keep mankind imprisoned and enslaved. If such people simply refused to follow immoral orders or refused to show up for work, the terror and violence against innocents would end in an instant.

Police brutality and official corruption are universal problems, regardless of what country you live in or what political philosophy you ally yourself with. It does not matter if you are a man or a woman, black or white, old or young, healthy or disabled. Even children still in the womb are in grave danger from these vicious brutes because pregnant women are another favorite target for their inhumanity.

Ask every good person you know to conduct rituals, spells, prayers and petitions to end this reign of terror. Let witchcraft become an influence in the world whereby individuals recognize their own power and work to attain justice each in their own way.

Perform your own spells to end official corruption and police brutality everywhere by destroying their power and inflicting the torment and pain they have caused others upon themselves, until they stop committing their crimes or suffer a just death.

Spell to End Police Brutality and Official Corruption

Conduct this spell to end police brutality and official corruption in your city or state. It is best performed on a Saturday at midnight, during a waning or new moon.

This spell should be done while taking all fire-safety precautions, either indoors in a fireplace or outdoors in a place where nothing can accidentally catch fire. Use a large cauldron or an old, tin coffee can placed on a heat-resistant base. You will need matches, nine feet of twine and some scissors.

Cut the twine into nine pieces of equal length. Then, hold them in your left hand and say aloud:

These are our enemies, the corrupt law enforcement agents and wicked judges of the world.

Then speak to them with great anger and

condemn them with these words, as follows:

From this moment on, you shall be haunted by the guilt of your misdeeds.
You shall feel the pain, death and indignation you have inflicted on others.
Likewise, you shall be tormented and suffer.
Now and forever more, you cannot sleep
Because your worst nightmares come alive before your eyes by night and day.
All you undertake turns to ashes.
Everything you touch rots and decays.
You are at the mercy of crushing waves.
Torrents of hail rain down on you from above.
Thunder and lightning crash all around you.
You are abandoned. You have no shelter and no refuge.
You are hopeless and suffer the just horror of a violent death,
Just as you have inflicted these terrors on others.
So be it, now and forever more. Amen!

Now, take a pair of scissors and cut their power by repeatedly cutting the twine into little pieces while saying:

Your power is cut. You no longer have the power to rob, rape, kill and destroy other people. You are weak and impotent.

Then, put the pieces of cord into the fire and let them burn to ashes as you say: *Now, you fall to ashes.*

Bury the remains in a graveyard.

The Power of Ogun

Ogun (pronounced oh-goon) is the powerful, primordial spirit of the Yoruba-speaking people of West Africa who is credited with inspiring the Haitian Revolution of 1805 and becoming "the most potent rallying force that drove the revolution."[11]

He is the spirit of rebellion against tyranny and oppression. Ogun is the master of weapons and fire who is syncretized with St. George the Dragonslayer who spoke out against oppression in Western Europe. He is a hunter, a healer and a valiant defender of the people who uses his machete to cut away darkness and deception and reveal the truth for all to see.

Ogun and fiery spirits like him from around the world have the power to help us heal and free us all from oppression. By forging a relationship with such spirits we learn to recognize our individual power to bring about justice in an unjust world.

PROBLEMS SURROUNDING YOUR HOME

Your home is your sanctuary or, at least, it should be. It is the one place you should be able to go, lock the doors and be able to find some peace and respite from the cares of the outside world. Unfortunately, your home can become fraught with terror, as well.

Marriages that go along without many problems for years can suddenly turn violent. Sociologists estimate that 1 to 3% of the population are psychopaths, although they vary widely in their estimation of the number of sociopaths with some guesses as low as 5% and others as high as 30%. How many people right now are unknowingly married to such a person?

Drugs are another problem that can creep in and

destroy your sanctuary. Over night, your quiet, peaceful neighborhood can be invaded by drug dealers. When the economy declines, crime becomes more prevalent and criminals more brazen. You can wake up one day to find that your formerly peaceful town has descended into a harrowing hell of violence.

If you rent, you may have problems with landlords who don't respect your privacy or who behave like creeps. Then, there are the problems of interfering in-laws and house guests who outstay their welcome.

The following spells will help you deal with such problems as these.

Bad Marriages

Frequently, people realize too late that they have entered into a bad marriage. Many times relationships work very well until the couple agree to sign a marriage license. Afterward, one party begins to believe they own and have the right to control the other. In the beginning, the abuse may be very subtle, for example, your partner may become critical, gradually exerting more control over you and eventually isolating you from your family and friends. At the next stage, the abuse can very quickly escalate to more overt types of abuses, including those of a financial, physical, sexual and psychological nature.

The moment you realize you have a problem, quietly get in contact with a good divorce lawyer and begin taking care of the financial part of things. Typically, once your partner gets the idea you want out, you can suddenly find yourself in even greater danger, both physically and in every other way. Therefore, be very discreet and call upon your inner actor. If you are in a situation where you fear for your safety, let all of your survival instincts kick into high gear.

While you are pondering your next move, appeal to the spirit world for help.

Spell to Stop an Abusive Man

If you are a woman in an abusive relationship with a man, you may perform this spell to get help from St. Rita, who is an advocate for women. It is best done on a Sunday, but you may do it any time as long as you do it in absolute secrecy.

If your husband is extremely controlling, you may have difficulty finding time alone. If possible, lock the door when you take a bath, taking care not to arouse his suspicions as you ask her for guidance and a peaceful end to your troubles.

You will need the following items:

Image of St. Rita or St. Rita medal
White pillar candle
Personal effects from the man
Small knife
Thorn or needle with which to make an inscription

Obtain a few of his hairs or nail clippings, then hollow out the bottom of the candle and place them inside. Inscribe your petition onto the side of the candle. For example, "St. Rita, stop his aggression against me" or "St. Rita, please, keep me safe and help me find a way out of this unfortunate union."

If you have a St. Rita medal or an image of her, place it by the candle. Then, light the candle and focus on what you want to happen. Let your emotions pour forth while you meditate on this. This spell can help keep things calmer until you have the opportunity to get out of the situation you find yourself in.

Once your petition is granted and you are safe, you must make a public announcement that St. Rita answered your prayers.

While St. Rita sometimes helps men, it is not a good idea for a man to use this spell because St. Rita favors women over men. She will work for a man, but he must be nearly perfect. Whenever she is invoked in a marriage, divorce often follows.

Old Fashioned Oil Lamp Spell
To Stop Violence in the Home

Vintage kerosene lamps are an elegant and cost-effective alternative to candles and may be used on an altar in place of a candle or alone in many of your spells. This spell is intended to stop another member of your household from injuring you, but if may be adopted to other types of situations in which someone close to you is aggressive toward you.

You will need the following items:

Old-fashioned kerosene or paraffin lamp
Vegetable-based lamp oil
Angelica root
Calamus root
High John the Conqueror root
Mud dauber dust (from an abandoned nest of this wasp-like insect)
Red pepper
Sugar
Un-laundered sock or underwear belonging to the person
Piece of parchment or plain white paper

Most of the ingredients in this spell are intended to cause confusion in the enemy, help you gain control over the situation and expedite a solution to your problem. The mud dauber dust is to tame and subdue the person. The sugar is to sweeten the person's attitude toward you.

Begin with a clean lamp and an empty oil compartment. Place the roots and a pinch each of mud dauber dust, red pepper and sugar into the oil font. Then cut approximately an inch square piece from the bottom of the sock or from the crotch of the underwear and place this into the oil chamber. Then, fill the rest of the chamber with vegetable-based lamp oil, which is available at many department stores and online.

As you place each of the items in the chamber, concentrate on your need for control over the situation. Place the lamp on your altar alone or before the image of spirits you work with and invoke their assistance. Then, write the following incantation on a small clean piece of parchment or white paper:

Dullix, ix, ux. Yea, you can't come over Pontio; Pontio is above Pilato. + + + [12]

Place your hands palms down over the items in the lamp and say these words aloud. Then make the sign of the cross three times. Afterward, keep the paper near you for protection.

Light the lamp, recite the incantation over it and allow it to burn for about an hour every night for nine nights. Afterward, light the lamp whenever you need protection. Keep the paper with the incantation written on it near you always.

Tips for using an old-fashioned oil lamp:

Roll the wick up and trim each of the corners slightly to keep the glass chimney from becoming blackened. Then, roll it down so that only 1/4 to 1/2 inches appears at the mouth of the burner. If you have just installed a new wick, wait a few hours before lighting it so it has time to soak up the oil.

After you light the wick, adjust the size of the flame by turning the knob on the side of the lamp.

Then, place the chimney on top.

Always treat oil lamps with the same caution you would use with candles. Place them on a stable surface where they will not be disturbed and do not leave them unattended. Refill the reservoir with oil frequently. Do not allow the oil to burn away completely.

To Control a Man or Woman by Magic

Get a small picture of the person. Anoint the edges of it with Controlling Oil and place it, face up, in the bottom of your right shoe to keep him or her under control.

Controlling Oil

4 oz. almond oil
3 T. clove
1 T. calamus root
1 T. dragon's blood resin
1 T. frankincense
2 tsp. damiana oil
7 drops bergamot oil

Spell to Stop Marital Rape

Marital rape is generally taken even less seriously than other types of sexual assault. But, having a rapist in your house that you cannot get rid of may very well be one of the most nightmarish situations you will ever have to deal with.

The following spell will put a damper on the rapists abilities. It is best performed on a Saturday during the waning or dark of the moon.

You will need the following items:

Black penis candle (or black taper)
Personal effect
Needle or thorn with which to make an inscription
2 T. saltpeter
2 T. chasteberry
3/4 cup olive oil (other oils will work, also)

Combine the saltpeter, chasteberry and oil into a small jar with a lid, shake it well and put it in a warm place. If possible, let the oil soak up the properties of the herbs for, at least, two weeks. Strain the oil through a piece of gauze or cheesecloth.

Obtain a personal effect such as a few pubic hairs, other hairs or bodily fluids of the person. Lightly melt the wax on the side of the candle and embed these items into the side of it.

Inscribe the following words onto the candle:

N., you are limp and powerless to do harm.

Anoint the candle with the oil using a motion away from you. Then, light it and focus on your desire.

When the candle has burned down, bury the refuse off your property to get rid of the person, in a cemetery to kill the person or place it in a tightly corked jar or bottle and throw it into a swiftly flowing river or stream to cause them to move far away from you.

Goofer Dust

Traditionally, this powder is put wherever the person has to walk through it. It causes extreme discomfort and is used to drive people away. Traditionally, to torment, poison and slowly kill your enemy, you sprinkle this powder where he or she must walk through it.

Obviously, it is ill-advised to sprinkle it inside or around your own house. Therefore, so you don't get into the stuff yourself, place a picture of your spouse in a box, then sprinkle some Goofer Dust on it. Tape the lid of the box securely, then bury it somewhere off your property, at a distant crossroad or in a cemetery.

This powder may be used in other spells to rid yourself of any unwanted person.

Goofer Dust

1 part graveyard dust (preferably taken from the grave of a murderer at midnight)
1 part sulphur
1 part ashes from a fire
1 part powdered bones (bone meal)
1 part powdered snake skin
1 part iron filings

This formula is designed to poison and eventually kill your enemy by means of magic, however, when it is blessed, placed in a small bag and carried with you, it becomes a protective agent.

Abusive spouses are another form of a bully. See, also, "Spells Against Bullies," below.

Bad Neighbors

If you live anywhere near other people long enough, you will probably be subjected to the problem of bad neighbors. Such people can sometimes become more than just a nuisance.

If you are dealing with noisy neighbors and you live in town, find out what ordinances exist, if any, with regard to noise pollution. If you live outside the city, there probably are no such laws.

As a rule, it is a bad idea to directly confront the noise-makers. To highlight this point, once an ex-Special Forces soldier who was well-trained for combat, received a concussion while politely asking the neighbors to turn down their stereo.

The most logical-seeming solution may be to call the police and ask them to talk to the offenders. But, this probably won't get you anywhere, either, and the police may label you as the neighborhood troublemaker, instead.

Fortunately, witchcraft can help you in this situation.

Drug Dealing Neighbors

There is now no place in the country, whether in the big cities or rural areas, that is safe from drugs and organized crime activities. If you live in the middle of the country, you may be subjected to the scourge of methamphetamine producers and dealers in once peaceful neighborhoods and rural areas. The problem is little known on either coast or in larger cities, but is a big problem in areas of the country, otherwise, generally regarded as safe.

Once there was a woman who lived alone in one such area of the country. This is what happened to her:

Some noise-makers moved into the house next door. At first, she thought it was just a bunch of rowdy kids. But, one day when they were trespassing on her property, she was able to get a good look at them and immediately realized that she was facing a much bigger problem. They were meth addicts! Shortly afterward, she began detecting the odors associated with the production of crystal meth. This is very dangerous to have near your home, not only because of the toxic fumes, but because of the possibility of an explosion.

She lived day and night with the chaos and fear of twenty to thirty people swarming in and out of the house next door. She dutifully contacted local law enforcement and made numerous, frantic calls to 911 because of fights and other illegal activities at the house. She made a daily practice of documenting the illegal activities.

By putting a little heat on them, she managed to force them to move the meth lab. But, right after that they began threatening her with rape in retaliation for having reported them to law enforcement.

One of her other neighbors called the police when she caught two of these depraved creatures trying to break into her house for the second time. But, law enforcement officers seemed not to take the robbery and the threats against this homeowner and others in the neighborhood very seriously, despite the rash of robberies in this previously crime-free area.

This situation culminated with the drug dealers trying to kill her, despite her months of attempts to get help through legal channels.

Most of the time law enforcement agents are powerless to help you, even if they really want to. Unfortunately, if you are dealing with a problem like this, you may have to take matters into your own hands in some way to save your life before it is all over. That is the sad truth.

Practical advice for anyone in this situation: Arm yourself and be prepared to defend yourself at all times. Never let your guard down for a split second. If you do not know how to handle a gun, you must learn. Document everything on the outside chance that law enforcement can help you and to legally protect yourself.

Be aware of the laws in your area. If you live some place where you are not allowed to protect yourself from rapists and killers who invade your home, you might want to consider making a plan to move somewhere else where your basic human rights are better respected.

Watch your mailbox. Drug dealers will steal your mail and you can become the victim of identity theft. Rent a private mail box elsewhere and stop receiving mail at your house. If this situation gets very bad, you won't be safe going to your mailbox, anyway. Do not take your trash out at night. Do not keep any kind of routine. If you have any decent neighbors, get to know them and encourage them to help you and each other.

That is the practical advice. Now, here is a way to metaphysically deal with this nightmare.

Spell to Make Bad Neighbors Move Away

Use this spell to make bad neighbors move away. An ideal time to perform it is on a Saturday during a waning moon.

You will need the following items:

Photograph of the house or the offenders
Piece of paper or parchment (optional)
Glass bottle with a cork or tightly fitting lid
Four Thieves' Vinegar (formula below)

If you know the neighbors' names, write them on a piece of paper or parchment. If you have an entire gang of drug dealers rotating in and out of the house, you probably will not have names. But, you can take a picture of the house or the offenders. If you have both names and a photograph, that is even better.

Roll up the photo and paper and place them inside the glass bottle. Fill it with Four Thieves' Vinegar. Then, cork it and seal it with warm wax or tighten the lid down completely.

When no one is looking, toss it into a body of

running water such as a river or stream. As the bottle is washed out to sea, visualize your enemy moving away from you.

Four Thieves' Vinegar

Place equal parts of the following dried or fresh herbs into a quart jar with a lid:

Lavender
Sage
Thyme
Melissa (lemon balm)
Hyssop
Peppermint
7 garlic cloves

Pour enough white or apple cider vinegar into the jar to soak the herbs, then pour in more so that the herbs sit in about the lower 1/3 of the jar and the other 2/3 of the volume of the jar is vinegar. Put a lid on it and shake it twice per day for two weeks. Store it in a warm place out of the direct rays of the sun. After two weeks, strain the liquid through a piece of cheesecloth or gauze and bottle your Four Thieves' Vinegar.

Psychic Vampirism to Drain Energy from Bad Neighbors

Having neighbors who conduct a 24-hour a day party, constantly fight with each other or who present a direct threat to your person or property can be very draining to you and, ultimately, detrimental to your health. You can stop the party and the fighting by draining the energy out of them and using it yourself. This is sometimes called psychic vampirism.

You may perform the following procedure with or without a crystal. You may find it helpful to hold a black obsidian or black tourmaline gemstone in your left hand to help you cleanse and purify their life energy as it flows to you. But, this can be done with a visualization, as well.

First, you must try to relax and concentrate. It is very important that for the duration of this operation that you do not allow yourself to feel any fear or frustration. Lie down and take two or three deep breaths.

Once you are relaxed, you must focus your mind on finding resonance with your subjects. Take them one at a time. If they are fighting or talking and you can hear their voices, this is enough to hone in on them.

Now, visualize them. It doesn't matter if this visualization is imperfect. See them in your mind. Then, imagine yourself plugging a big cord into the region just above one of the subjects' tailbone. This is a powerful energy center, which is used both by healers and black magicians. It adjusts the flow of life energy into the entire body.

Imagine yourself plugging into this energy center just like you would plug a cord into the wall. Then, siphon the energy off very quickly. Done properly, this can cause a fast drop in blood pressure. When it is done by healers, it is done very gently. But, your purpose is to stop these people who are making your life miserable, if not impossible. So, do it vigorously. You can even open up this center, visually widening it to several inches, then see the energy coming out and forming in a large ball at your left hand.

See this energy ball in your left hand very vividly. If you are holding a black crystal, allow the energy from the crystal to infuse the ball of light. See it being cleansed. If it was dark or gray before, it is now crystal clear with a tinge of blue. Allow it to come up your left arm and use it to energize your entire body.

Do this to each individual in the party who is causing trouble. If you do this correctly, in a matter of minutes, you should hear the noise cease entirely. They will become exhausted or ill and you will feel better because you have their energy. This method works very well, but you may have to do it on several occasions before they get the message.

This technique, also, works well on amateur musicians who like to play their drums and guitars so the entire neighborhood can hear. Simply, zone in on one musician at a time, then drain and siphon off his energy. Usually, they will stop playing in a matter of seconds.

Classic Remedy for Bad Neighbors: Hot Foot Powder

Hot Foot Powder laid down where the enemy has to walk through it is a classic Hoodoo method for getting rid of unwanted people. Sprinkle it where the person lives, works or must walk through it. Alternatively, use it in spells by applying it to objects that represent the person you want to get rid of.

The main ingredient in Hot Foot Powder is graveyard dirt, preferably gathered at midnight from the grave of a murderer.

Hot Foot Powder

1 cup graveyard dirt
1 tsp. sea salt
1 tsp. red chili pepper
1 tsp. black pepper
1 tsp. cayenne pepper
1 tsp. sulfur
1 tsp. High John the Conquer root (powdered)

Traditionally, Hot Foot Powder is laid down secretly. This is the safest method, however, an alternative method worked well for a couple who were plagued by noisy, dangerous neighbors. But, it will probably only work if you are big and intimidating-looking.

The husband became angry when the neighbors were throwing yet another wild drug party. He took a bottle of Hot Foot Powder in a glass jar and broke it on their porch while cursing at them. They became quiet very quickly and the next day, they fled the neighborhood never to return.

On a side note, bad people seem to respond to bad smells. Creating an unpleasant stench around their dwelling may encourage them to leave.

You may, also, ask for assistance from Santa Muerte, the Intranquil Spirit or some other frightening and potentially unpleasant spirits who may be dispatched to torment your enemy and force them to do your will.

Always be aware of the laws and the nature of law enforcement in your area. What you will find in most places is that the cops won't do anything to the bad guys. Once you have established what they will and won't do to them, you will have a better idea of what you can do in your own self-defense.

Creepy Landlords

This is a very big problem for women who rent a house or apartment. Sometimes creepy landlords go so far as to peep through your windows, place cameras in your bedroom or bathroom, or barge in on you when they know you are sleeping. Usually, as a renter in such a situation, you are locked into a lease or you may have no place else to move to.

Creepy landlords are potentially very dangerous people. It is not wise to stay in an apartment where you are afraid of someone associated with the place doing you harm. Unfortunately, if you are in a dangerous situation with a landlord, you must weigh the value of your personal safety against the importance of your credit rating, if you break a lease. The credit rating has been the instrument of abusers for far too long! Don't over-estimate its importance.

There is usually no point in involving law enforcement unless you can prove something. For instance, there are numerous cases where tenants have actually located a video camera in their bedrooms or bathrooms. In such instances, you have may have proof of a crime, however, it is usually your word against his and you are going to lose every time because no one will believe you.

In most cases, all you can do is appeal to the spirit world for protection while you plan a course of action to escape your unfortunate housing situation.

Fiery Wall of Protection Spell

To surround yourself with an impenetrable wall of psychic protection, perform this candle burning spell, preferably on a Tuesday or Thursday during a full moon.

You will need the following items:

White or black candle
Fiery Wall of Protection Oil (formula below)

Anoint the candle with Fiery Wall of Protection Oil, then light the candle and say:

Forged in fire and born in the flame,
No evil shall come here to harm or maim.
None shall penetrate this fiery wall,
Which surrounds me now and protects us all.
So be it! Amen.

As you cast this spell, visualize a strong, impenetrable wall of fire and flames surrounding you.

Fiery Wall of Protection Oil

Grind equal parts of the following ingredients in a mortar and pestle and add them to 4 ounces of almond oil.

2 T. dragon's blood
1 T. sea salt
2 T. cinnamon
1 T. ginger

Allow the herbs to soak in the oil for, at least, two weeks to reach maximum potency.

Spiritually Contaminated Places

Sometimes a dwelling simply has a bad feeling or a bad spirit about it, which can cause you to feel uneasy.

A woman once rented an apartment next to a friend of hers. During the first few weeks in her new home, she began having the most horrific, very realistic nightmares. These were so real that she wasn't sure if she was a wake or asleep. One of the strangest characteristics of the nightmares was the realistic sensation of being pulled by her legs up into the air.

She told her friend that she was having these terrible nightmares about being dragged and tortured. That is when her friend told her that the apartment had once been the residence of a mutual acquaintance of theirs who had barely survived being abducted from that apartment by her boyfriend and another man, robbed, raped and left for dead. She managed somehow to survive, but was in very poor health. This apartment was the one she was living in with her boyfriend when the incident happened.

If you are living in an apartment, house or other dwelling where you are experiencing violent nightmares, this is a sign that something bad may have taken place there and the energy from it is lingering. It must be spiritually cleansed, sometimes multiple times, to get rid of the problem.

White Sage and Sweet Grass to Purge Unwholesome Energies

Smudge your home white white sage and sweet grass to purge unwholesome energies and encourage beneficial spirits.

Begin by lighting a bundle of white sage. Then, walk from room to room commanding the negative energies and bad spirits to leave while allowing the smoke to drift into every nook and cranny. Then, repeat this procedure with a braid of sweet grass as you invite friendly spirits back.

With your index finger, trace a pentagram in the air as a protective shield on every door, window, fireplace or other opening to the outside.

Smudging does not work in every instance. If the spirits or energies in the house are of a more stubborn nature, you will have to try a different procedure.

If you suspect you are dealing with something demonic, call upon the archangel Michael to protect your home. Light a red candle and visualize Michael with his sword, driving away the evil spirits. Then ask for his protection. He will place his angelic soldiers all around your home. Let this vision be so powerful that you can see them with your mind's eye.

Troublesome In-laws

In contrast to some of the previously addressed problems, interfering in-laws who do not respect you or your role in your own home seem like a minor issue. But, they can be a pernicious problem and the cause of marital discord.

In these instances, your in-laws may be creating a divide, either intentionally or unintentionally, between you and your spouse. You must get him or her on your side and renew your loyalty and devotion to each other. For this, you may perform this simple spell.

You will need the following items:

Hairs from your spouse's head
Hairs from your own head
Whole High John the Conqueror root
Red mojo bag
Thyme
Rosemary

Acquire some of your spouse's hair and some of your own from a hairbrush or comb. Rub them together between your palms to create an interlocked fiber. Place this in a red mojo bag with a sprinkle each of thyme and rosemary. Add a whole High John the Conqueror root to this bag to regain mastery over your relationship and your household.

Keep this bag with you. Carry it near your heart or in your front pocket.

If you have the additional problem of your in-laws staying at your house and you want to get them out, perform a spell to get rid of unwanted house guests.

To Get Rid of Unwanted House Guests

To get rid of unwanted house guests, including the in-laws, you may use the same procedure as in the "Spell to Make Bad Neighbors Move Away" in which you place a photograph, their signatures, a strip of their un-laundered socks or underwear in a corked and sealed bottle with Four Thieves' Vinegar. Then, toss it into a fast-moving body of water.

Alternatively, place a boiled egg under their bed. They will move out very soon.

You may, also, sprinkle salt in their shoes and imagine them walking away.

Crossroad Spell to Banish House Guests

For the best results, perform this spell on a Saturday night, during a waning moon to get rid of unwanted house guests of any kind.

You will need the following items:

Black candle
Cauldron or fire-safe container
Asafoetida
Red pepper seeds
Nettles (to irritate them and hasten their departure)
Small piece of parchment or piece of clean, white paper
Personal effect or photograph of the unwanted guests
Mortar and pestle
Small bag of any kind

Obtain a personal effect from each guest you wish to banish. This may include a photograph, signature, hairs, nail clippings or a strip of unlaundered underwear or socks.

Light the black candle

Write the following incantation and symbols on the parchment:

+ + + *Flee, devil and take thy servants with you!* + + +

In the cauldron or other fire-safe container, burn the personal effect to ashes. Then, recite the incantation three times, crossing yourself for each "+." Then, burn the paper. Allow the candle to burn out completely while meditating on your desire for the people to leave your home.

Then, put the ashes and two or three tablespoons of each of the herbs, asafoetida, red pepper seeds and dried nettles into the mortar and pestle and grind them together. Place this mixture into a small bag.

Afterward, plot a path of four-way crossroads from your house that leads away from your home beginning with the one nearest to you and leading far out of town. Drive this path, placing a small sprinkle of this mixture at each crossroad repeating the incantation and crossing yourself each time.

8

PROBLEMS AT YOUR WORKPLACE OR SCHOOL

Workplaces and schools are often the source of discord. They may be fraught with sources of distress including bullies, gossips, control freaks, bad bosses and co-workers, insensitive classmates and even incidents of assault and violence.

Many people suffer in silence, having no viable recourse – at least, not in the physical world.

The following spells and procedures are intended to help you deal with such problems.

Bullies

Many people remember going to school with a bully and the problem of bullying is commonly associated with school children. But unfortunately, children who bully often grow up to be adults who bully. Therefore, this problem does not automatically go away once you leave school.

Bullying takes on many different forms, all of which can be psychologically harmful to the victims; sometimes it escalates to physical violence against them. Therefore, it should be taken seriously, however, laws, policies and official complaint procedures often do little or nothing to address the problem.

In fact, sometimes reporting a bully causes their aggression to escalate and creates more problems for the victim. If you report being bullied to your school administrators, you may be regarded as the trouble-maker instead of the bully. Similarly, if you report a bully to your employers, you may risk losing your job. If the bully happens to be a teacher, administrator or work supervisor, you may have an even more difficult problem.

In the broadest sense of the term, bullies include a variety of other types of malefactors discussed in previous chapters, including abusive spouses, creepy landlords, unscrupulous financiers, corrupt members of law enforcement and common criminals.

White light practitioners will tell you to send your enemies love or send them the color pink. When that fails – and it will – try the following method for dealing with all kinds of bullies.

The Employment of Demonic Spirits

Conjure a spirit to torment the evil-doer until he or she does what you want them to do. Choose an unpleasant spirit from the Goetia or other powerful grimoires and command him to seek revenge on bullies, stop them from causing harm and bring them under your will. For instance, you might choose Vepar, Sabnok, Malphas or Andromalius from the book, *The Goetia: The Lesser Key of Solomon the King,* by S. L. MacGregor Mathers and Aleister Crowley.

Vepar appears in the shape of a mermaid, with the power to cause death in the course of three days by means of parasites; he, also, has the power to heal the same.

Sabnok appears as an armed soldier with a lion's head, riding on a pale horse. He has the power to wound an enemy and cause him to be afflicted by festering sores and parasites. This spirit, also, provides conjurers with good familiars to aide them in any endeavor.

Malphas appears as a crow before shifting to a human form. He speaks in a hoarse voice and can bring you information about your enemies, which you can use against them. He, also, provides good familiars to assist you in your work.

Andromalius appears as a man holding a serpent. He brings back thieves and punishes them and other wicked people.

These four spirits are only examples of the demons you can conjure to assist you in obtaining revenge, forcing a bully, stalker or abuser to submit to your will, putting an end to harassment of any kind, placing an enemy out of your way or altering the outcome of an event. Some spirits specialize in bringing down the powerful and destroying their structures, sowing discord among your enemies, gaining the favor of those in powerful positions and assisting you in a wide variety of endeavors.

You may choose any spirit according to your needs. Once you have summoned a spirit for the first time, obtain from him an agreement that he will come to you immediately whenever you call him. If the spirit gives good familiars, ask for such spirits to serve you for any purpose you require.

Then, on any day except the 2nd, 4th, 6th, 9th, 10th, 12th or 14th day of a new moon, do the following:

Cast a circle about nine feet in diameter with a triangle formed outside of it, at least, three feet on each side, in which the entity shall appear. This circle and triangle do not need to be created in any elaborate ceremony and may be simply marked off with masking tape. You may place a mirror or a bowl of water inside this triangle along with a drawing of the spirit's corresponding sigil from *The Goetia*. Bring a ritual sword or athame and a pentacle inside the circle with you to show the spirit and command him when he appears.

Do not over-complicate the ritualistic aspects of summoning, but be persistent in reciting the conjurations. Visualize the circle you are standing in and the triangle in their three-dimensional geometric forms. Before you begin your conjurations of the spirit, accumulate the etheric force within yourself. Disperse the accumulated and condensed etheric energy inside the orb (or geometric cone, if you prefer to see it that way) and three-sided pyramid. See this energy flowing out of you and into the confines of these geometric forms. Spend a few minutes doing this before you begin the first conjuration and repeat this meditation procedure to recharge the circle and triangle as you feel it is necessary.

Always address and command the entity from within the safety of your circle. If you must step outside the circle for any reason, always recite the

License to Depart, then wait a few minutes before leaving the circle.

This method is the authors own; another far more elaborate method for preparing the circle and triangle is given in *The Goetia*. The original conjurations for these spirits are powerful and may be adapted to conjure other demonic entities and gain their obedience.

The First Conjuration

I invoke and conjure thee, O Spirit N., and, fortified with the power of the Supreme Majesty, I strongly command thee by BARALAMENSIS, BALDACHIENSIS, PAUMACHIE, APOLORESEDES and the most potent princes GENIO, LIACHIDE, Ministers of the Tartarean Seat, chief princes of the seat of APOLOGIA in the ninth region; I exorcise and command thee, O Spirit N., by Him Who spake and it was done, by the Most Holy and glorious Names ADONAI, EL, ELOHIM, ELOHE, ZEBAOTH, ELION, ESCHERCE, JAH, TETRAGRAMMATON, SADAI: do thou forthwith appear and shew thyself unto me, here before this circle, in a fair and human shape, without any deformity or horror; do thou come forthwith, from whatever part of the world, and make rational answers to my questions; come presently, come visibly, come affably, manifest that which I desire, being conjured by the Name of the Eternal, Living and True God, HELIOREM; I conjure thee, also, by the particular and true Name of thy God to whom thou owest thine obedience; by the name of the King who rules over thee, do thou come without tarrying; come, fulfil my desires; persist unto the end, according, to mine intentions.

I conjure thee by Him to Whom all creatures are obedient, by this ineffable Name, TETRAGRAMMATON JEHOVAH, by which the elements are overthrown, the air is shaken, the sea turns back, the fire is generated, the earth moves and all the hosts of things celestial, of things terrestrial, of things infernal, do tremble and are confounded together; speak unto me visibly and affably in a clear, intelligible voice, free from ambiguity. Come therefore in the name ADONAI ZEBAOTH; come, why dost thou tarry? ADONAI SADAY, King of kings, commands thee.

If necessary, repeat this conjuration several times until you perceive the spirit in the triangle. At any point during the course of these conjurations when the spirit appears, make your communications with him, conduct your business and afterward give him license to depart as instructed below.

But, if this conjuration fails to bring a manifestation, accumulate the etheric force within you and disperse it into the circle and triangle before proceeding to the next conjuration.

Second Conjuration

I invoke, conjure and command thee, O Spirit N., to appear and shew thyself visibly before this circle, in fair and comely shape, without deformity or guile, by the Name Of ON; by the Name Y and V, which Adam heard and spake; by the Name Of JOTH, which Jacob learned from the Angel on the night of his wresting and was delivered from the hands of his brother Esau; by the Name of God AGLA, which Lot heard and was saved with his family; by the Name ANEHEXETON, which Aaron spake and was made wise; by the Name SCHEMES AMATHIA, which Joshua invoked and the Sun stayed upon his course; by the Name EMMANUEL, which the three children, Shadrach, Meshach and Abednego, chanted in the midst of the fiery furnace, and they were delivered; by the Name ALPHA and OMEGA, which Daniel uttered, and destroyed Bel and the Dragon; by the Name ZEBAOTH, which Moses named, and all the rivers and waters in the land of Egypt brought forth frogs, which ascended into the houses of the Egyptians, destroying all things; by the Name ESCERCHIE ARISTON, which, also, Moses named, and the rivers and waters in the land of Egypt were turned into blood; by the Name ELION, on which Moses called, and there fell a great hail, such as never was seen since the creation of the world; by the Name ADONAI, which Moses named, and there came up locusts over all the land of Egypt and devoured what the hail had left; by the Name HAGIOS, by the Seal of ADONAI, by those others, which are JETROS, ATHENOROS, PARACLETUS; by the three Holy and Secret Names, AGLA, ON, TETRAGRAMMATON; by the dreadful Day of Judgment; by the changing Sea of Glass which is before the face of the Divine Majesty, mighty and powerful; by the four beasts before the Throne, having eyes before and behind; by the fire which is about the Throne, by the Holy Angels of Heaven, by the Highly Wisdom of God; by the Seat of BASDATHEA, by this Name PRIMEMATUM, which Moses named, and the earth opened and swallowed Corah, Dathan and Abiram; do thou make faithful answers unto all my demands, and perform all my desires, so far as thine office shall permit. Come therefore peaceably and affably;

come visibly and without delay; manifest that which I desire; speak with a clear and intelligible voice, that I may understand thee.

If the spirit still fails to manifest after reciting this conjuration several times, again, fill the circle and triangle with the etheric force and proceed to the next conjuration.

Third Conjuration

I conjure thee, O spirit N., by all the most glorious and efficacious Names of the Great and Incomparable Lord the God of Hosts, come quickly and without delay, front whatsoever part of the world thou art in; make rational answers to my demands; come visibly, speak affably, speak intelligibly to my understanding. I conjure and constrain thee, O Spirit N., by all the aforesaid Names, as, also, by those seven other Names wherewith Solomon bound thee and thy fellows in the brazen vessels to wit, ADONAI, PRERAI, TETRAGRAMMATON, ANEXHEXETON, INESSENSATOAL, PATHUMATON and ITEMON; do thou manifest before this circle, fulfil my will in all things that may seem good to me. Be disobedient, refuse to come, and by the power of the Supreme Being, the everlasting Lord, that God Who created thee and me, the whole world, with all contained therein, in the space of six days; by EYE, by SARAY, by the virtue of the Name PRIMEMATUM, which commands the whole host of Heaven; be disobedient, and behold I will curse and deceive thee of thine office, thy joy and thy place; I will bind thee in the depths of the bottomless pit, there to remain until the Day of the

Last judgment. I will chain thee in the Lake of Eternal Fire, in the Lake of Fire and Brimstone, unless thou come quickly, appearing before this circle, to do my will Come, therefore, in the Holy Names ADONAI, ZEBAOTH, AMIORAM; come, ADONAI commands thee.

If the spirit still fails to appear, then he has been dispatched by his commander, the King, therefore, invoke the King and command him to send him to you, as follows:

Invocation of the King

O thou great and powerful King AMAYMON, Who rulest by the power of the Supreme God, EL, over all Spirits, superior and inferior, but especially over the Infernal Order in the Dominion of the East, I invoke and command thee by the particular and true Name of God, by the God Whom thou dost worship, by the Seal of thy creation, O the most mighty and powerful Name of God, JEHOVAH, TETRAGRAMMATON, Who cast thee out of Heaven with the rest of the Infernal Spirits; by all the other potent and great Names of God, Creator of Heaven, Earth and Hell, of all contained therein; by their powers and virtues; by the Name PRIMEMATUM, which commands the whole host of Heaven. Do thou force and compel the Spirit N. here before this circle, in a fair and comely shape, without injury to myself or to any creature, that he may give me true and faithful answer, so that I may accomplish my desired end, whatsoever it be, provided that it is proper to his office, by the power of God, EL, Who hath created and doth dispose of all things, celestial, aërial, terrestrial and infernal.

After you have recited this invocation two or three times, again, conjure the spirit beginning with the the First Conjuration. If he does not come, he is bound in Hell and must be released from his chains using the following conjuration:

The Chain Curse

O thou wicked and disobedient N., because thou hast not obeyed or regarded the words which I have rehearsed, the glorious and incomprehensible Names of the true God, Maker of all things in the world, now I, by the power of these Names, which no creature can resist, do curse thee into the depths of the Bottomless Pit, to remain until the Day of Doom, in the Hell of unquenchable fire and brimstone, unless thou shalt forthwith appear in this triangle, before this circle, to do my will. Come, therefore, quickly and peaceably, by the Names ADONAI, ZEBAOTH, ADONAI, AMIORAM. Come, come, ADONAI, King, of commands thee.

If he still does not manifest, draw his seal from the book, *The Goetia*, on a piece of clean parchment, place it in a black box along with sulphur, asafoetida, some aloes, wormwood and valerian root. Bind the box with iron wire, then hang it on the point of your ritual sword or knife and, while facing eastward, hold it over hot coals as you say:

Fire, I conjure thee, O Fire, by Him Who made thee, and all other creatures in the world, to torment, burn, and consume this Spirit N. everlastingly.

N., because thou art disobedient, and obeyst not my commandments nor the precepts of the Lord thy God, now I, who am the servant of the Most High and Imperial Lord God of Hosts, JEHOVAH, having His celestial power and permission, for this thine averseness and contempt, thy great disobedience and rebellion, will excommunicate thee, will destroy thy name and seal, which I have in this box, will burn them with unquenchable fire and bury them in unending oblivion, unless thou comest immediately, visibly and affably, here before this circle, within this triangle, assuming a fair and comely form, without doing harm unto myself or any creature whatsoever, but giving, reasonable answer to m requests and performing, my desire in all things.

If the spirit still does not appear, say:

Thou art still pernicious and disobedient, willing not to appear and inform me upon that which I desire to know; now therefore, in the Name and by the power and dignity of the Omnipotent and Immortal Lord God of Hosts, JEHOVAH TETRAGRAMMATON, sole Creator of Heaven, Earth and Hell, with all contained therein, the marvellous Disposer of all things visible and invisible, I do hereby curse and deprive thee of all thine office, power and place; I bind thee in the depth of the Bottomless Pit, there to remain unto the Day of judgment, in the Lake of Fire and Brimstone, prepared for the rebellious Spirits. May all the Company of Heaven curse thee; may the Sun, the Moon, the Stars, the Light of the Hosts of

Heaven, curse thee into fire unquenchable, into torments unspeakable; and even as thy name and seal are bound up in this box, to be choked with sulphureous and stinking substances and to burn in this material fire, so, in the Name of JEHOVAH, and by the power and dignity of the three Names, TETRAGRAMMATON, ANEXHEXETON, PRIMEMATUM, may all these drive thee, O thou disobedient Spirit N., into the Lake of Fire, prepared for the damned and accursed Spirits, there to remain until the Day of Doom, remembered no more before the face of that God Who shall come to judge the quick and the dead, with the whole world, by fire.

Threaten the spirit by placing the box in the flame, whereupon he will appear. When he does, quench the fire, burn a little incense and show him the image of a pentacle as you say:

Behold thy confusion, if thou be disobedient. Behold the Pentacle of Solomon which I have brought into thy presence. Behold the person of the Exorcist, who is called OCTINIMOES, in the midst of the Exorcism, armed by God and fearless, potently invoking and calling. Make, therefore, reasonable answers to my demands; be obedient to me, thy Master, in the Name of the Lord BATHAL, rushing upon ABRAC, ABEOR, coming upon BEROR.

At this point, he will become obedient and bid you to ask whatever you wish because this is the order of things and it is his purpose to serve you. When he manifests and his meek and humble in your presence, say:

Welcome, Spirit (or, most noble King), welcome art thou unto me; I have called through Him Who created Heaven, Earth and Hell, with all contained therein, and thou hast obeyed, also, by the like power. I bind thee to remain affably and visibly before this circle, within this triangle, so long as I need thee, to depart not without my license, till thou hast truly and faithfully fulfilled all that I shall require.

Conduct your business with the spirit. For instance, make your commands, request any information you desire, obtain familiar spirits to serve you and make your agreements with him. Once you have your agreement with the spirit to appear when you call him, you may obtain his services at any time.

After you have finished your communications, bid him to go in peace by reciting the License to Depart.

License to Depart

O Spirit N., because thou hast diligently answered my demands, I do hereby license thee to depart, without injury to man or beast. Depart, I say, and be thou willing and ready to come, whensoever duly exorcised and con red by the Sacred Rites of Magic. I conjure thee to withdraw peaceably and quietly, and may the peace of God continue for ever between me and thee. Amen.

Once you have recited the License to Depart, do not step outside the circle until you are certain he has departed. Continue to meditate in the circle for a few minutes to allow the spirit time enough to leave.

Other Techniques of Employing Demonic Entities and Imps

You may dispatch demonic entities or imps, which are lesser demonic entities and thought-forms, to an enemy psychically by going through the preceding conjurations mentally.

Also, if you have a well-developed psychic sense and can detect demonic entities or thought-forms obsessing or infesting another person, you may mentally remove them and send them to cling to your enemies instead.

When you do this, instruct the entities, commanding them to do specific things to your enemy. For example, entities can be called upon to cause nightmares, drain your enemy's life force, cause thoughts of suicide and promote bad luck. If you are plagued by a group of bullies send demonic forces to cause them to fight among one another.

Whenever your enemies cause you trouble, curse them in this way. Also, curse them at night while they sleep and their defenses are down. If they drink or do drugs, curse them at times when you believe they are under the influence because, at such times, their defenses will be very low.

Once you have completed your ritual either physically or mentally, leave all thoughts of it behind you. Focus on raising your own vibratory rate. Literally, you must think happy thoughts. Sing and dance. Do whatever makes you happy. This is a simple method of preventing the lower vibrations you sent out from finding resonance with you, if any should try to return to you. Although, as long as the entity is happily feeding on one of your enemies, it is not likely to bother you.

The employment of demonic entities works with all kinds of bullies including abusive partners, conniving relatives, evil schoolmates, bad administrators, cruel co-workers, stalkers and corrupt government agents. All such evil-doers can be dominated or eliminated by this method.

Spell to Protect Children from Bullies

If your child is being bullied at school, consider how to get him or her out of there as soon as possible. Do not wait for teachers or administrators to take responsibility. More often than not they blame and punish the victim instead. Meanwhile, your child is suffering and may be in danger.

As you sort out your practical plan of action, metaphysically protect your child with this spell.

You will need the following items:

Poppet
9 pink candles
9 small, clear quartz crystals
Personal effects of the child
Lavender
Chamomile
Rose petals
Clover
Angelica
Elecampane
Mugwort
Small pink cloth

Make or purchase a poppet. These are featureless rag dolls usually made of muslin, which can be found at hobby or craft stores. Fill it with any combination of protective herbs from the above list. Add a few of your child's hairs or nail clippings.

Place the poppet on your altar and arrange nine pink candles in a circle around it. Set a crystal in between each candle.

Then, as you light each candle, say:

Guardian spirits, protect my child with light and love. Spirits of vengeance, guard my child and strike down all enemies who conspire against him (or her).

Envision a pink cloud enveloping the poppet and radiating a protective glow. See your child surrounded by guardians, both those who bring love and peace as well as those who strike at enemies.

When the candles have burned down. Wrap the poppet in a pink cloth and place it in a drawer where it will be safe.

To Stop Gossiping Co-workers or School Mates

To silence gossips, perform the Beef Tongue Spell from *Chapter 6*. Alternatively, you may use this spell to sweeten your enemy's words.

You will need the following items:

Brown candle
Needle or thorn with which to make an inscription
Piece of paper or parchment
Honey

Inscribe the gossipers' names on the brown candle. Then, on a piece of paper write:

Your words about me will only be sweet.

Dribble honey on the paper, fold it in half twice and place it beneath the candle. Light the candle and concentrate on your desires for nine consecutive nights.

On the tenth night, bury the refuse where it won't be found.

San Ramón Nonnato to Silence Your Enemies

San Ramón Nonnato (Saint Raymond Nonnatus) who was previously mentioned in *Chapter 5. Police Brutality, Official Corruption and Theft During Travel,* is not only called upon for invisibility, but to stop gossip. According to a popular legend, when he was imprisoned by the Moors, San Ramón was silenced by his jailers who drove holes into his lips and affixed a padlock to his mouth.

To call upon San Ramón to silence your enemies, obtain a prayer card of him and place a red candle before it, at least once per week. Recite the prayer to San Ramón and petition him to silence your enemy, for example, say, "San Ramón, I ask you to shut the mouth of N." Then affix a penny to the mouth of the image of San Ramón using a piece of adhesive tape or chewing gum.

Spell to Stop a Gossip

This is a very therapeutic and effective spell to stop a gossip or other troublemaker. It is best begun on the night of a new or waning moon, preferably on a Saturday.

You will need the following items:

Cheap ceramic figurine to represent your enemy
Vines with thorns
Several feet of black ribbon or black cord
Hammer
Small, sturdy box
Packing tape
Graveyard Dirt, Goofer Dust or Hot Foot Powder

Hold the figurine in your hand as you say, "I name thee, N." Then, taking care not to scratch yourself, wrap it in thorny vines and tie them with a piece of ribbon or cord. Put it in the box. Sprinkle it with the dirt, dust or powder. Close the box, wrap it securely with packing tape, then tie it with cord or ribbon.

With the hammer in your hand, speak to the person (figurine) in your angriest voice and tell them what you want them to do, for example, "Shut up!" Strike the box three times. Do it hard enough to break the figurine inside. Each day for nine days in a row, talk to the figurine inside the box just as you did before and strike the box three times with your hammer.

On the ninth day, bury the battered box in a deep hole, if possible, in a cemetery.

Classic Bend Over Spell

Use this spell to get control over a person who is making your life miserable and bend them to your will.

You will need the following items:

Black image candle to represent your subject
Needle or thorn with which to make an inscription
Personal effect
Paper
Red ink pen
Bend Over Oil (formula below)
Bend Over Powder (formula below)

Write your enemy's name in a column nine times on the paper, then turn it 90 degrees and cross and cover over it completely it by writing the words, "Bend over," nine times.

Inscribe the name of your enemy on the candle. Carve out the bottom of the candle and insert a small photograph of him or her, a signature, some hair or fingernail clippings. Anoint the candle with Bend Over Oil and rub it in, using a twisting motion, as you project your desires onto the candle. Envision what you want the person to do and how you want them to behave toward you.

Place the candle on its holder. Dip the four

corners of the paper into the Bend Over Oil, then sprinkle it with Bend Over Powder. Fold the paper toward you twice, enfolding the powder in the middle. Imagine your desired outcome as you do so. Turn the paper 90 degrees and fold it once or twice more. Then, place it beneath the candle holder.

Sprinkle Bend Over Powder around the candle. Light it and let it burn all the way down. Bury the remains near the subject's home or business and forget about it.

Bend Over Powder

Combine equal parts of the following:

Allspice
Calamus root
Cinnamon

Bend Over Oil

To make the oil, combine the above powdered herbs in a lidded jar, then cover them three times over with almond oil. Keep the jar in a warm place for two weeks, shaking it once or twice per day. Then, strain and bottle it. For extra strength add a few drops of bergamot and vanilla oils.

Black Coffin Death Spell

If your enemy is making your life so miserable that you see no other way to end, use this spell to eliminate him or her by means of malefic witchcraft. This spell is best performed on a Saturday night during a new or waning moon.

You will need the following items:

Black candle
Needle or thorn with which to make an inscription
Black candle wax (softened) or clay
Small piece of parchment or white paper
Dark Arts Oil (formula below)

Using softened, black candle wax or clay, fashion an image of your enemy and a coffin big enough to lay it in.

Inscribe the name of your enemy and the word, "Die," nine times on the side of the candle, then anoint it with Dark Arts Oil.

Take the little figure in your left hand and speak to it, as follows:

I name you N. Your days are numbered, you son-of-a-bitch! You are going to die.

Feel free to improvise when you speak this command. Then, rub the figure and the coffin with Dark Arts Oil. Write your enemy's name on a piece of paper and place it in the coffin. Form a lid over the top.

Concentrate on your enemy meeting a violent death, perhaps at the hands of a random killer or in a terrible accident. If he is a chronic trouble-maker, he may very soon fall on his own sword. Allow the candle to burn down completely.

After midnight, bury the remains of the candle, the coffin and its contents nine inches deep in an old cemetery.

Dark Arts Oil

4 oz. almond oil
Pinch of black pepper
2 pinches of valerian root
3 black dog hairs
Pinch of mullein
Pinch of sulphur

Combine these ingredients together in a bottle with a tightly-fitting lid. This potion will attain its full potency after about two weeks.

Separation Spell

On a softer note, if two or more people are conspiring against you and you want to cause discord between them, conduct a spell of separation. This spell may be used whenever you want to break apart any relationship.

This spell is best begun on a Saturday night during a waning moon.

You will need the following items:

Black figure candle for each person
Needle or thorn with which to make an inscription
Separation Oil
Separation Powder

Procure a black figure candle for each person who is the subject of this spell.

Write each person's name on one of the candles, then anoint them with Separation Oil. Arrange the candles with about an inch between them, facing outward.

Sprinkle Separation Powder in a circle around the candles and say:

Once thick as thieves, now bitter as bile. No more unity, only enmity between N. and N. You get on each others nerves and in each others hair. You hate each other and now you separate and depart from each other. So be it!

Let the candles burn for a little while before snuffing them out.

Perform this ceremony for nine consecutive nights. Move the candles a little further away from each other every time you do it. At the end of this spell, when the candles have burned down completely, take the refuse and bury it at a distant crossroad or in a cemetery.

If it is possible, sprinkle Separation Powder or Oil where the subjects must walk through it or come in contact with it. Be subtle.

Separation Oil

4 oz. almond oil
1 tsp. chili powder
1 tsp. cinnamon powder
1 tsp. low John root powder
1 tsp. ground black pepper
1 tsp. iron filings
1 tsp. vetivert powder

Separation Powder

To make the powder, combine equal parts of the above dry ingredients without the oil. You may add this to a base of rice powder or corn starch to thin it out and make it easier to handle.

A Word on Performing Work or School-related Spells

Whenever you conduct spells for problems related to your work or school, you must be especially discreet. Schools and workplace authorities have become increasingly paranoid and the spell will likely be ruined in more ways than one if anyone finds out what you are up to.

When you perform a spell against a school or workplace bully, never do it at those locations. Instead, do it in the privacy of your own home or some other appropriate place. Keep all spell related items and amulets securely hidden inside your clothing.

Where witchcraft is concerned, secrecy is power.

DEALING WITH TRAUMA
IN THE AFTERMATH

The only reason you need spells of revenge and protection is because grave wrongs have been done to you or you are being threatened by other people. If volatile situations emerge frequently or drag on over a period of time, you can become traumatized in various ways. This can lead to a state of severe anxiety, which is now called Post-traumatic Stress Disorder (P.T.S.D.). Although, it is not really a disorder, at all; rather, it is a sign that your memory works very well.

In order to go on with your life in a harmonious way, you will need to restore your sense of safety. It is necessary for you to be in a situation where you are no longer being exposed to any on-going trauma before you can really begin healing.

For example, if you are still in danger from a

stalker or if you have reason to fear retribution from a criminal you have successfully prosecuted, you should take every physical precaution you can. Fortify your home or, if the situation is very extreme, seek refuge away from home. Never rely on law enforcement agents to protect you. Even if they wanted to, they can't.

If you have ever had to deal with something like this, you know the truth. Your problem will be convincing the people around you, who have not had the same experiences and who often cannot tell the difference between reality and what happens in movies.

If you are able to, gather good, supportive people around you.

Unfortunately, all too often in the aftermath of some horror, you will find that your friends are quick to turn their backs on you. The more serious the crimes committed against you, the more likely you are to be abandoned or abused by other people. In cases where you are nearly murdered, you have lost a child to violence, you have been raped or you are being pursued by a gang of stalkers, you will probably look around and find that you are completely friendless.

This is because most people either cannot deal with reality or they are completely lacking in empathy for others. The only way they can understand the reality of a situation like this is if it happens to them. Until then, it's not their problem – it's yours – and in their own minds, they will devise every reason why you are to blame. They will tell themselves – and you – that such things would never happen to them because they are smarter, holier or in some other way superior to you. At these times, you will hear the most horrible things imaginable come out of their mouths.

This is why many victims of violent crimes and rape, in particular, frequently find themselves completely isolated. In cases of severe trauma, people become uncomfortable leaving their homes because being away from other people who constantly re-traumatize them with their words and actions is a far better option than being in their company.

Of course, the conventional alternative is professional counseling. Armchair experts and television talk show hosts tell you that you should talk about your problems, if not with a friend, then with a therapist. The problem with this is that your friends and your therapist will probably only make things worse for you. Some professionals are now admitting what the rest of us have known all along: If you suffer from severe anxiety as a result of violence, talking about it can trigger severe anxiety attacks and actually impede the healing process.

With or without the support of others, you must establish peace and tranquility in your life. Then, the healing can begin.

Make use of all of these spells for protection and healing that suit your needs.

A Ritual Bath to Exorcise Unwholesome Entities and Restore Peace of Mind

This is an excellent ritual to perform before conducting any spell, any time you feel out of sorts, when you have difficulty sleeping or if you are experiencing nightmares. It comes from Dion Fortune's book, *Psychic Self-defense*, which is a very good handbook on this subject.

These prayers are used for the blessing of the

salt and water to be used in a bath, to drive away evil by making the cross on the forehead and for sprinkling inside or outside of any place that requires exorcism and protection from evil. Place an amount of salt and water in separate dishes and perform the prayers as follows:

In each place below where you see the symbol, "(+)," make the sign of the cross like Catholics do. A similar crossing is used in the rituals of The Hermetic Order of the Golden Dawn to which Dion Fortune belonged. Aleister Crowley's Thelemites use a similar crossing with a minor variation.

When pointing, extend your index and middle finger. Your ring and pinkie fingers should be bent backward toward the palm with the thumb resting upon their nails. When extending your hand over the water and salt, your palm should be facing downward, parallel to the surface, your fingers extending outward flatly with your thumb held rigidly at a right angle to the forefinger.

Pointing at the salt, say: *I exorcise thee, creature of earth, by the living God (+), by the holy God (+), by the omnipotent God (+), that thou mayest be purified of all evil influences in the Name of Adonai, Who is Lord of Angels and of men.*

Extending your hand over the salt, say: *Creature of earth, adore thy Creator. In the Name of God the Father Almighty, maker of heaven and earth, and of Jesus Christ His Son, our Saviour, I consecrate thee (+) to the service of God, in the Name of the Father and of the Son and of the Holy Ghost. Amen.*

Pointing at the water, say: *I exorcise thee, creature of water, by the living God (+), by the Holy God (+) by the omnipotent God (+), that thou mayest be purified from all evil influences in the Name of Elohim Sabbaoth, Who is Lord of Angels and of men.*

Extending your hand over the water, say: *Creature of water, adore thy Creator. In the Name of God the Father Almighty, Who decreed a firmament in the midst of the waters, and of Jesus Christ His Son our Saviour, I consecrate thee (+) to the service of God, in the Name of the Father and of the Son and of the Holy Ghost. Amen.*

At this point, you may set aside a portion of the blessed salt and water for house sprinkling before proceeding.

Then, casting the salt into the water, say: *We pray Thee, O God, Lord of Heaven and earth, and of all that in them is, both visible and invisible, that Thou mayest stretch forth the right hand of Thy power upon these creatures of the elements and hallow them in Thy Holy Name. Grant that this salt may make for health of body and this water for health of soul, and that there may be banished from the place where they are used every power of adversity and every illusion and artifice of evil, for the sake of Jesus Christ our Saviour. Amen.*

To consecrate the combined salt and water, extend your hand over it and say: *In the Name which is above every other name, and in the power of the Father and of the Son and of the Holy Ghost, I exorcise all influences and seeds of evil; I lay upon them the spell of Christ's Holy Church, that they may be bound fast as with chains and cast into outer darkness, that they trouble not the servants of God.*[13]

When you bless the water and salt for use in a bath, you may add a few drops of rosemary and lavender essential oils to the water to enhance its soothing and healing powers.

Healing from the Loss of an Unborn Child

When men rape and batter women, they do it for their own personal gratification and because women are inhuman objects to them. But, an assault on a woman can be an assault on an unborn child and, in fact, life itself. This is something there may never be any complete healing from and many women suffer in silence.

When a human life has been destroyed, it cannot be replaced and the horrifying ordeal of giving birth to a dead child is one that cannot be forgotten. May anyone who tells you to forgive rapists and child-killers rot in a grave along side them forever!

You can speak to the spirit of your child and he or she can speak to you. Sometimes this comes in dreams, but, at times when you are very still, you will feel the child's presence.

Let the spirit of the child know he or she is welcome in your house by giving them a small memorial. It doesn't need to be anything ostentatious that would attract unwanted attention from guests, but it should be given a place of honor in your home. It can be a simple urn. Fill it angelica root, lavender, rosemary and other fragrant herbs. Add some rose and clear quartz crystals.

Then, light a white candle and say:

I consecrate this urn to you, N., You are always welcome in my home and wherever I may be. You will forever be a member of my family. I will be with you and you will be with me. So be it!

You may use this little spell to help heal from the loss of a child, regardless of the cause.

Restoring Your Health

When people have been physically injured or severely emotionally traumatized, they need more than just spiritual healing; they need physical healing, too. Over time, the trauma caused by the original injuries can erode a person's health. It can cause graying hair, heart disease, cancer and a host of other diseases.

Victims of extreme violence or other severe trauma sometimes only live a few years after their ordeal before dying of cardiovascular disease or cancer. Therefore, if you are a survivor, you must take particular care of your health.

It is important to take care of yourself, eat well and supplement your diet with vitamins, minerals and herbs so your body can properly heal itself. If you have been severely injured or disabled by your attacker, a program of physical therapy may help you resume your former level of activity.

Raw juicing is a powerful method for restoring health. For extra nutritional support during or after a period of stress, the B Vitamins, particularly B-6, B-12, and Vitamin C are especially important and the herbs rhodiola, licorice and ginseng may be helpful for recovery. Sources of iodine such as nettles and seaweed in your diet help support the thymus (the master adrenal gland).

Onions and garlic are powerful adrenal supporting foods. Chop a whole onion and two cloves of fresh garlic and sautee them in a tablespoon of olive or coconut oil. This simple combination can provide remarkable improvements in cases of adrenal fatigue, which is characterized by severe exhaustion that is not remedied by sleep.

The book, *Magical Healing: How to Use Your Mind to Heal Yourself and Others*, by this author describes techniques for discharging unhealthy, depleted bioplasmic energy and replacing it with healthy, vibrant vital energy. Meditation and energy manipulation is a remarkably effective method of restoring the body's subtle energy intake centers, which are associated with the adrenal glands, to proper functioning.

Increase your vital energy by meditating with a crystal ball or crystal skull. Larger crystals tend to have more of this energy than smaller ones. Interestingly, reconstituted crystal balls sometimes have even more energy than natural ones, but every piece of quartz is different. Test the energy of the crystal by holding it in your left hand or placing your left palm directly over it. A strong crystal will impart an electrical charge that you can feel running into your hand and up your arm.

Every kind of quartz crystal has its own special healing ability. The following are examples of gemstones, which are especially helpful for healing from trauma:

Clear and rutilated quartz crystals: To increase the body's vital force and for any purpose.

Rose quartz: For emotional healing.

Black obsidian: To destroy negative energies.

Amethyst: For anxiety.

Red jasper: For restoring the vital force.

Lapis lazuli: To generate and maintain the supply of vital force. It is commonly worn by healers. The blue-tinged field it emits has a stabilizing effect on the subtle energy bodies.

Tie a piece of red cord or yarn around your waist, neck or left wrist to prevent the loss of vital energy. This will, also, provide a measure of protection against psychic vampires, the evil eye and black magicians.

Call upon spirits, such as Santa Muerte, St. Barbara, the Orisha Chango or the Norse god Thor, for help with matters of healing and rejuvenation.

Valerian Root for Anxiety

Valerian is one of the best herbs for dealing with severe anxiety. If you have difficulty sleeping because of tension or frequent nightmares, this root can help.

Make a powerful decoction of the freshest dried Valerian root you can find. Mexican grocery stores are a good source, but any herb shop is likely to have some on hand.

Place two teaspoons of ground root or a large, single piece of root into boiling water. Add two or three pinches of lemongrass for taste and enhanced relaxation power. Let it cook down for four to five minutes. If you are using one of the large roots, put it aside and let it air dry; it may be used twice in a decoction before it begins to lose its power.

Let this brew cool for a few minutes. Then, strain the liquid into a cup. Add sugar or honey to taste, if you like. Drink this before bed time. It will help you a little on the first night. But, when you do it the second night, you should have a very good sleep and awake feeling rested and very relaxed.

A little powdered ginger from your cupboard, made into a tea by adding one to two teaspoons to boiling water can sometimes bring immediate relief of insomnia, too.

Always heed all cautions with regard to herbs and use only as directed. As always, if you take pharmaceutical drugs or are under the care of a physician, seek his or her advice before making any changes in your diet.

Once you are sufficiently calm, again, and able to focus, try using self-hypnosis by making your own recordings. This can help you to regain control over certain aspects of your life, again. It is simply a way of talking to your subconscious mind, re-programming it however you want it to be, using your own voice in a recording. You may, also, use pre-recorded hypnosis tapes.

Putting Your Financial Life Back Together

Any severe emotional and psychological trauma or physical disability can make it difficult to work. And, unless you can identify your attackers and managed to get the whole thing on video, you probably won't have much of a chance in the court system. Few people ever receive a settlement after an injury by law enforcement agents and if you are injured by a private individual, you probably have even less of a chance of being compensated.

Most people who are injured in an assault of any kind have to be responsible for their own medical and other bills and suffer in silence with the consequences for the rest of their lives.

Fortunately, there are new opportunities for you to work from home these days. Often people who are injured become work-at-home freelancers at whatever they do. If you have any kind of writing or web design skills, graphics design, sales, marketing, accounting or bookkeeping skills, you can turn this into an independent venture of your own.

Calling on St. Jude for Financial Help

Call upon St. Jude for help with money issues. Acquire a green St. Jude candle. Anoint it with cinnamon or rue essential oil.

Make the sign of the cross. Then, say the following:

St. Jude, glorious apostle, faithful servant and friend of Jesus, the name of the person who betrayed our Lord has caused you to be forgotten by many, but the true Church invokes you as the patron of things despaired of. Pray for me, who is so miserable; pray for me, that I may finally receive the consolations and the succor of Heaven in all my necessities, tribulations, and sufferings, in particular [Insert your petition here] and that I may bless God with the Elect throughout Eternity.

Again, make the sign of the cross. Then, light the candle and meditate upon your desires. Do this for nine days in a row.

Ask the spirit of St. Jude for guidance in financial matters and ask to be shown and given opportunities. When St. Jude has satisfied your request, it is customary to make a public announcement thanking him for his help or to make a small donation to a charity in his name.

You may, also, call upon many other spirits who

specialize in assisting with financial matters, such as Santa Muerte, who is a powerful ally in the acquisition and protection of money and wealth.

MEASUREMENT CONVERSIONS AND ABBREVIATIONS

Abbreviation Key for Measurements

T. = Tablespoon
tsp. = teaspoon
oz. = ounce
g = gram
ml = milliliter

Conversion of Measurements

3 tsp. = 1 T.
1 cup = 16 T.
1 cup = 8 oz.
1 pint = 16 oz.
1 pint = 2 cups

1 tsp. = approximately 4.2 g
1 cup liquid = approximately 220 to 240 g
1 cup non-liquid = approximately 120 to 140 g
1 dram = 1/8 oz. = 60 grams = 3.697 ml = 60 drops
1 dram = .125 fl. oz. or approximately 3/4 tsp.
1 pint = approximately 473 ml
1 ml = 15 drops of liquid

REFERENCES

1. Leland, Charles G., *Etruscan Roman Remains in Popular Tradition*, 1892. P. 332.

2. Ibid.

3. Evans-Pritchard, E. E., *Witchcraft, Oracles and Magic Among the Azande*, Oxford at the Clarenden Press, 1937, P. 82.

4. Colpitts, Mike, *Mortgage Fraud Led by California, Florida, Arizona and Nevada, Housing Predictor*. March 25, 2011. Retrieved March 25, 2011. http://www.housingpredictor.com/2011/mortgage-fraud-sunbelt-states.html

5. DiGregorio, Sophia, *Traditional Witches' Formulary and Potion-making Guide: Recipes for Magical Oils, Powders and Other Potions*, Winter Tempest Books, 2011.

6. Cooper, Barry, *Police Are Twice As Likely To Sexually Assault You And Five Times As Likely To Murder You*, Retrieved April 2, 2011. http://nevergetbusted.com/2010/articles/police-twice-as-likely-to-murder

7. "Constitution-free Zone Map," *ACLU*. Retrieved on March 20, 2011. http://www.aclu.org/constitution-free-zone-map

8. DiGregorio, Sophia, *Traditional Witches' Formulary and Potion-making Guide: Recipes for Magical Oils, Powders and Other Potions*, Winter Tempest Books, 2011.

9. *Lucky Mojo Curio Company* [correspondence], Christopher Warnock. Lucky Mojo. April 27, 2000 Retrieved: March 19, 2011.
http://www.luckymojo.com/esoteric/occultism/magic/folk/hoodoo/cy200005lawkeepaway.txt

10. Wippler, Gonzalez Migene, *The New Revised 6th & 7th Books of Moses and the Magical Uses of the Psalms, Original Publications*, New York, 1982. P. 174.

11. Ogen, Olukoya, *Historicizing African Contributions to the Emancipation Movement: The Haitian Revolution*, 1791-1805. [Text of a paper slated for presentation during the conference on "Teaching and Propagating African History and Culture to the Diaspora and Teaching Diaspora History and Culture to Africa.] Retrieved March 20, 2011.
http://eprints.soas.ac.uk/5684/2/TheHaitianRevolution1791-1805.pdf

12. Hoffman, John George, *Pow-Wows, or Long Lost Friend*, 1820.

13. Fortune, Dion, *Psychic Self-defense*, 1930.

ABOUT THE AUTHOR

Angela Kaelin is the author of metaphysical books, such as, *How to Read the Tarot for Fun, Profit and Psychic Development for Beginners and Advanced Readers*, *The Traditional Witches' Book of Love Spells*, *Spells for Money and Wealth*, and *Magical Healing: How to Use Your Mind to Heal Yourself and Others*. She is, also, an alternative health writer and the author of *All Natural Dental Remedies: Herbs and Home Remedies to Heal Your Teeth & Naturally Restore Tooth Enamel*.

MORE WINTER TEMPEST BOOKS

If you enjoyed this book, you might enjoy other Winter Tempest Books:

All Natural Dental Remedies: Herbs and Home Remedies to Heal Your Teeth & Naturally Restore Tooth Enamel by Angela Kaelin

Blood and Black Roses: A Dark Bouquet of Vampires, Romance and Horror by Sophia diGregorio (Fiction)

The Devil's Grimoire: A System of Psychic Attack by Moribus Mortlock

The Forgotten: The Vampire Prince by Sophia diGregorio (Fiction)

Grimoire of Santa Muerte: Spells and Rituals of Most Holy Death, the Unofficial Saint of Mexico by Sophia diGregorio

How to Communicate with Spirits: Séances, Ouija Boards and Summoning by Angela Kaelin

How to Develop Advanced Psychic Abilities: Obtain Information about the Past, Present and Future Through Clairvoyance by Sophia diGregorio

How to Read the Tarot for Fun, Profit and Psychic Development for Beginners and Advanced Readers by Angela Kaelin

How to Write Your Own Spells for Any Purpose and Make Them Work by Sophia diGregorio

Magical Healing: How to Use Your Mind to Heal Yourself and Others by Angela Kaelin

Natural Remedies for Reversing Gray Hair: Nutrition and Herbs for Anti-aging and Optimum Health by Thomas W. Xander

Practical Black Magic: How to Hex and Curse Your Enemies by Sophia diGregorio

Spells for Money and Wealth by Angela Kaelin

To Conjure the Perfect Man by Sophia diGregorio (Fiction)

The Traditional Witches' Book of Love Spells by Angela Kaelin

BLACK MAGIC FOR DARK TIMES

Traditional Witches' Formulary and Potion-making Guide: Recipes for Magical Oils, Powders and Other Potions by Sophia diGregorio

Disclaimer: The author and publisher of this guide has used her best efforts in preparing this document. The author makes no representation or warranties with respect to the accuracy, applicability, fitness or completeness of the contents of this document. The author disclaims any warranties expressed or implied. The author of this book is not a medical or legal professional and is not qualified to give medical or legal advice. Nothing in this document should be construed as medical or legal advice. The material in this book is presented for informational purposes only. The procedures described in this book should not be used a substitute for treatment from state approved, licensed medical authorities.

Nothing in this book should be construed as incitement to dangerous or illegal acts and the reader is advised to be aware of and heed all pertinent laws in his or her city, state, country or other jurisdiction. Any medical or legal questions should be addressed to the proper medical or legal authorities. The author shall in no event be held liable for any losses or damages, including but not limited to special, incidental, consequential or other damages incurred by the use of this information. Always take proper precautions with candles, sharp objects, essential oils, herbs and use only as directed.

The statements in this book have not been evaluated by any other government entity. The statements contained herein represent the legally protected opinions of the author and are presented for informational purposes only. Anyone who uses any of the information in the book does so at their own risk with the understanding that the author cannot be held responsible for the consequences.

FTC Disclaimer: The author has no connection to nor was paid by any brand or product described in this document with the exception of any other books mentioned which were written by the author or published by Winter Tempest Books.

Copyright: This document contains material protected under copyright laws. Any unauthorized reprint, transmission or resale of this material without the express permission of the author is strictly prohibited.

Printed in Great Britain
by Amazon.co.uk, Ltd.,
Marston Gate.